The Kingdom of Auschwitz

ALSO BY OTTO FRIEDRICH

The Poor in Spirit
The Loner
Decline and Fall
Before the Deluge: A Portrait of Berlin in the 1920's
The Rose Garden
Going Crazy: A Personal Inquiry
Clover: A Love Story
The End of the World: A History
City of Nets: A Portrait of Hollywood in the 1940's
Glenn Gould: A Life and Variations
The Grave of Alice B. Toklas
Olympia: Paris in the Age of Manet

The Kingdom
of Auschwitz

Otto Friedrich

HarperPerennial
A Division of HarperCollinsPublishers

To Mala Zimetbaum

HarperCollins books may be purchased for educational, business, or sales promotional use. For information please write Special Markets Department, HarperCollins Publishers, Inc., 10 East 53rd Street, New York, NY 10022.

FIRST EDITION

Designed by Nancy Singer

Library of Congress Cataloging-in-Publication Data

Friedrich, Otto, 1929–
The kingdom of Auschwitz / by Otto Friedrich.
   p. cm.
"The Kingdom of Auschwitz appeared in the Atlantic monthly in somewhat condensed form"—T.p. verso.
Includes bibliographical references.
ISBN 0-06-097640-3
1. Auschwitz (Poland: Concentration camp) 2. Holocaust, Jewish (1939–1945)—Poland. 3. Holocaust, Jewish (1939–1945)—Poland—Personal narratives. I. Title.
D805.P7F74   1994
940.53'174386—dc20   94-14752

11 ❖ / RRD(H) 30 29 28 27 26 25 24

Contents

Maps appear on pages xv and xvi.

Preface

Fully fifty years have passed since German forces evacuated the ruins of the concentration camp at Auschwitz, abandoning hopelessly ill prisoners to their illnesses and driving thousands of emaciated survivors westward into the snow. Yet the place still haunts the imagination. The images of Auschwitz, the encircling networks of barbed wire, the squat gray guard towers, the railroad tracks to nowhere, all evoke the modern sense of hell. Dante's description of the gate to the inferno recorded a message of utter despair: *"Lasciate ogne speranza, voi ch'intrate."* (Abandon all hope, ye who enter here.) The gate to Auschwitz offered a message of false hope, all the more hellish for its mocking mendacity: *"Arbeit macht frei."* (Work brings freedom.)

Some philosophical souls like to argue that quantity makes no difference in questions of good and evil. One life is just as sacred as a hundred, and therefore one killing is just as iniquitous as a massacre. This is not true. If it were just a question of cruelty and suffering, concentration camps like Ohrdruf, Woebblin, Nordhausen, Gusen, or Thekla might be just as infamous as Auschwitz, and yet they are all but forgotten. The Holocaust still horrifies us not because some Jews were murdered—that happens almost every week in New York City—but because the incredible total of six million murders represents the attempt to kill *all* Jews: genocide. And Auschwitz represents the Holocaust, more than such sinister installations as Majdanek or Sobibor, largely because more people died here than anywhere else. Here death not only became a way of life but expressed that way of life by all the methods of mass production. Everything that man has learned from technology he applied here to the destruction of life. This was the worst that has ever happened.

Perhaps the most terrible single fact about Auschwitz is that nobody knows, even to the nearest hundred thousand, exactly how many people died there. Commandant Rudolf Hoess acknowledged at his trial after the war that he had been responsible for the slaughter of 2.5 million, plus "another half million who succumbed to starvation and disease." But then he added: "I myself never knew the total number and I have nothing to help me make an estimate of it." He said that he got the figure of 2.5 million from his friend and confederate Adolf Eichmann, but he said that it seemed to him "far too high"; and at his trial he reduced it to 1,135,000. Having begun by keeping detailed records of all the killings, the Nazis ended by trying to destroy all their records, and so the dead remained uncounted. The scholars working at the Auschwitz Museum long estimated the total at 4 million, but this did not go unchallenged by various so-called "revisionists" and by more serious analysts as well. Gerald Reitlinger argued in *The Final Solution* that the total was less than 1 million, and that both Hoess and Eichmann had been "boasting" in their higher estimates. In the spring of 1990, the Auschwitz Museum's senior historian, Franciszek Piper, released the results of a ten-year study suggesting that the total of those who died at Auschwitz amounted to a little more than 1 million, about the same that Hoess had finally testified. Amid all this confusion, the consensus now seems to be 1.5 million. Thus more than 2 million once-mourned victims have mysteriously disappeared, another illustration of the general ignorance.

The place itself is now falling into a sorry state of dilapidation. Of the three hundred-odd wooden barracks in Auschwitz-Birkenau, the adjacent camp where most of the killing took place, only eighteen remain standing in a row, and some of those are falling in ruins, their doors knocked off their hinges, their floorboards rotting away. The surrounding grass and weeds grow waist high. To many survivors, Polish officials, and well-wishers, something should be done about this, some restoration that would preserve the dignity of the site. "If nothing is done, the place will simply fall apart," said Kalman Sultanik, vice president of the World Jewish Congress.

Efforts toward this restoration encounter many difficulties, starting with the condition of the camp itself. "Everything was poorly made," according to one Polish official, "—the barracks, the crematoriums, the paper used for documents. It is difficult to preserve something that was made to vanish." Then comes the inevitable problem of money. A team of experts from the Metropolitan Museum in New York estimated that long-term preservation of the site would require

$42 million. Who has $42 million, and who, having $42 million, wants to spend it on something as grim as that? A fund-raising drive nonetheless started, and various fund-owners were cajoled into pledging donations. The German government, almost inevitably, felt most of the pressure and did most of the pledging, a total of $20 million that it too would probably rather spend on something like social welfare or farm subsidies or even refurbishing the Sans Souci Palace of Frederick the Great. The Israelis pledged a more or less symbolic $100,000.

Not everyone was convinced, though, that a restoration of Auschwitz was in itself a good thing. "There are many who feel the camp should be reconstructed to its original state," said Bohdan Rymaszewski, secretary of the International Committee of the Auschwitz Museum. "In my opinion this would be nothing other than forgery." Even what little has been done strikes some as a jarring contradiction of what took place. "The grass in the women's camp had recently been cut, giving the rows of one-story brick barracks an almost suburban look . . . " a *New Yorker* correspondent named Timothy W. Ryback wrote after a recent visit to Auschwitz. "The ramp, like the rail line, has been flawlessly restored. In the afternoon sun, the newly laid gravel glints like a seaside beach . . . "

Even if such restorations were perfect, some would challenge the results. Jean-Claude Pressac, a French Holocaust expert, thinks visitors should be herded through a restored gas chamber so that they would get the "slap in the face" necessary to show them "that this was insane and criminal." George S. Wheeler, a restoration specialist at the Metropolitan Museum in New York, strongly disagrees. "For me it's almost voyeuristic to recreate a gas chamber," he told the *New York Times.* "You're playing to a voyeuristic public, and it has very questionable motives." James Young, professor of English and Judaic studies at the University of Massachusetts, argues that the relics of Auschwitz should simply be allowed to age "gracefully."

The sharpest controversy over the preservation of Auschwitz has pitted various Jewish groups against the Catholic Church. At the center of the conflict was the establishment in 1984 of a Carmelite convent in an Auschwitz building that had once been used to store Zyklon B poison gas. The Carmelites said they wanted only to offer silent prayers for all those who had died at Auschwitz. Jewish groups that keep an eye on such things were quick to protest that the Carmelites were trying to "Christianize" Auschwitz, to obscure the fact that the overwhelming majority of victims had been Jews, killed because they were Jews, that Auschwitz was in effect a uniquely Jewish catastrophe, not to be mourned by Christians. The Carmelites could have answered—but didn't—that thousands of Christians also died at Auschwitz, and that they also deserved to be commemorated. Instead, they simply said that they wanted to pray for all the victims, Jew and gentile alike.

This was perfectly acceptable under Christian doctrine, but it violated some very hardy Jewish traditions. One was the collective memory of brutally forced conversions; another was the belief that "assimilation" meant the obliteration of Jewish identity. More specifically, and in more recent times, many Jews could remember that anti-Semitism was ingrained in many Poles, and that the Vatican had done little to prevent or resist the Holocaust. Indeed, the Jews commonly thought of their persecutors as "the Christians," though neither the Nazis nor their gentile victims would ever have applied that term to the perpetrators of the Holocaust. The Polish view of all these questions was passionately different from that of the

Jews. It regarded Nazi genocide as aimed against Poles quite as much as against Jews, and it regarded the Vatican as a sturdy ally in the Polish struggle for freedom. It was therefore quite natural for the Communist government of Poland to erect plaques at Auschwitz declaring that "four million people . . . suffered and died here at the hands of the Nazi murderers." There were some who felt deeply offended, however, that the victims had been described as "people" rather than as Jews.

And for anyone who suspected the Catholic Church of generally trying to control everything within its reach, there was something particularly suspicious about the church's interest in canonizing whatever Christian martyrs it could find in the ruins of Auschwitz. One of the first of these was Edith Stein, a German Jewish philosopher who took the name of Sister Teresia a Crusia when she became a Carmelite nun. She was abducted from a Carmelite convent in the Netherlands and gassed at Auschwitz in 1942. When the Polish Pope John Paul II announced her beatification in 1987, he said that she had "offered herself to God as a sacrifice . . . for her threatened and humiliated Jewish people."

No soothing words like those could cool the Jewish determination to get the Carmelite convent with its 23-foot wooden cross out of Auschwitz. In 1987, an agreement was finally negotiated in Geneva by four European cardinals and Theo Klein, president of the European Jewish Congress. It reassuringly promised that Auschwitz "remains eternally the symbolic place of the Shoah, which arose from the Nazi aim of destroying the Jewish people. . . ." But it spoke just as warmly of "the sufferings of the Polish nation." The main point, though, was that the Catholics agreed to move the Carmelites out of Auschwitz by February of 1989 and into a nearby center for Christian-Jewish dialogue.

After two years of peace, it turned out that the Carmelites had not moved by the agreed deadline, and that the construction of the new center for Christian-Jewish dialogue had not even begun. In May of 1989, about 300 Jewish women staged a protest march outside the convent. The Carmelites ignored them. In July, Jewish students staged a similar march. They carried banners saying, "Carmelites, leave Auschwitz." They were harassed by local residents and workmen, who shouted slogans like "Back to Palestine." A few days later, an assertive rabbi from New York led another protest march. When his followers were barred at the gate, they clambered over the fence. The rabbi piously denied any violent intent. "When our attempts at opening a dialogue were ignored," he said later, "we scaled the fence, wrapped ourselves in our prayer shawls, and sang and studied Torah on the convent porch. . . . Soon after we commenced our peaceful demonstration, workers from inside the convent threw buckets of water mixed with urine and paint over our heads. Several hours later, they attacked again, this time kicking and punching us. . . . Their leader yelled, 'Heil Hitler!' Nuns peered through the convent windows as we were beaten. . . ."

Franciszek Cardinal Macharski of Cracow, one of the signers of the Geneva agreement to move the Carmelites, now repudiated the agreement on the ground that the Jews had been "aggressive." Jozef Cardinal Glemp, primate of Poland, went even further. He not only declared that the Poles could not afford the $2 million that the proposed center for Christian-Jewish dialogue would cost but he called the Geneva agreement "offensive." "It's a scandal to expel the nuns from the convent," he said. "Jews have to understand that dedicating their lives in prayer near the place where Christians were martyred does not offend their feelings."

As an added touch, Glemp blamed the whole controversy

on the Jews. "Do you, esteemed Jews, not see that your pro-
nouncements against the nuns offend the feelings of all
Poles?"

Whatever the Jewish answer might be, Glemp provided
an answer of his own: "Dear Jews, do not talk with us from
the position of a people raised above all others and do not
dictate conditions that are impossible to fulfill."

The Jewish view that only Jews had died at Auschwitz
was quite wrong, and offensive too, but Glemp's counter-
arguments echoed a traditional Polish anti-Semitism that the
Polish Pope now considered unacceptable. And so the Vatican soon issued a statement declaring that the Geneva agreement would be honored and the Carmelites would depart
from Auschwitz, one of these days. And so both sides lapsed
into sullen silence, each viewing the compromise as victory.
What both had forgotten in their blind pride was that
Auschwitz could never be fittingly commemorated unless it
remained forever free from violence and coercion.

For this new edition of *The Kingdom of Auschwitz* I have made
some corrections and additions in my original text and
updated the "Note on Sources."

Locust Valley, New York
April 1994

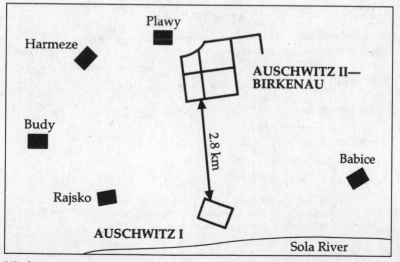

Work sites surrounding the Auschwitz I and Auschwitz II.

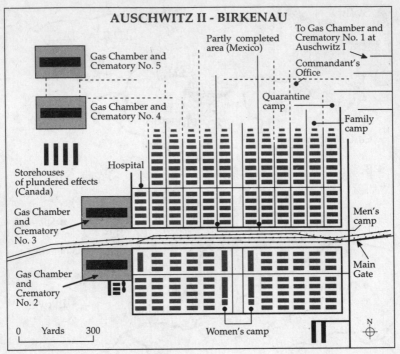

Plan of Auschwitz II–Birkenau.

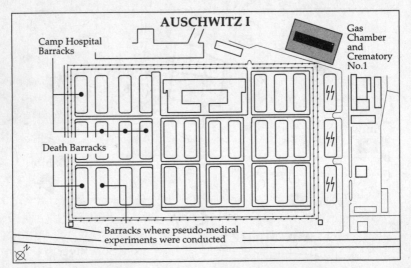

Plan of Auschwitz I.

The Kingdom of Auschwitz

"A large, heavy guard prowling outside brutally snatched it away from me. 'Warum?' I asked him in my poor German. 'Hier ist kein warum,' (there is no why here) he replied, pushing me inside with a shove."

—Primo Levi, *Survival in Auschwitz*

In a remote corner of southern Poland, in a marshy valley where the Sola River flows into the Vistula about thirty miles west of Cracow, Heinrich Himmler decided in the spring of 1940 to build a new prison camp. The site chosen by some of his underlings had little to recommend it. Outside a bleak little town named Oswiecim, there stood an abandoned Austrian artillery barracks, a collection of about twenty single-story brick buildings, most of them dark and dirty. The surrounding countryside in the foothills of the

Carpathians was strangely beautiful, a mosaic of meadows speckled with wild flowers, but a committee of Himmler's adjutants reported back to Berlin that the prospects for a large prison camp were forbidding. The water supply was polluted, and there were mosquitoes everywhere, and the barracks themselves were virtually useless.

Himmler was undaunted. In this first year of the subjugation of Poland, the need for new detention camps to help establish German law and order in the east was overwhelming. One of Himmler's most dedicated subordinates, SS Major Rudolf Hoess, commandant of the "protective custody camp" at Sachsenhausen, differed from his skeptical colleagues. He reported to Berlin that hard work could transform the marshes along the Vistula into a valuable outpost of the Reich. The place had two important qualities: it had good railroad connections, but it was isolated from outside observation. Himmler promptly assigned Hoess to take charge of the project. On April 29, 1940, Hoess and five other SS officers from Sachsenhausen descended from the Breslau train and surveyed the prospect before them. "It was far away, in the back of beyond, in Poland," Hoess later recalled in the memoir that he wrote shortly before he was hanged in 1947. The Poles called the place Oswiecim; the Germans called it Auschwitz.

Hoess was a remarkable man, as anyone who confesses to personal responsibility for the death of about three million people presumably must be. It was he, apparently, who devised the famous steel sign that mockingly welcomed the trainloads of prisoners to Auschwitz: *Arbeit Macht Frei*. Work makes you free. He seems not to have intended it as a mockery, nor even to have intended it literally, as a false promise that those who worked to exhaustion would eventually be released, but rather as a kind of mystical declaration that self-sacrifice in the form of endless labor does in itself bring a kind of spiritual freedom. "All my life I have thoroughly enjoyed working," Hoess wrote on the eve of his hanging. "I have done plenty of hard, physical work, under the severest conditions, in the coal mines, in oil refineries, and in brick-yards. I have felled timbers, cut railroad ties, and stacked peat. . . . Work in prison [is] a means of training for those prisoners who are fundamentally unstable and who need to learn the meaning of endurance and perseverance. . . ."

He was not a mere brute. One of the few surviving photographs shows a man with a high forehead, large, searching eyes, a full-lipped and rather prissy mouth. His devout parents had been determined that he should become a priest. His father and his grandfather had been soldiers, and though the father retired from the Army to become a salesman in Baden-Baden, he passed on to his only son his belief in military discipline. And piety. He took his son on pilgrimages to shrines as far away as Einsiedeln and Lourdes. "I was taught," Hoess wrote, "that my highest duty was to help those in need. It was constantly impressed on me in forceful terms that I must obey promptly the wishes and commands of my parents, teachers and priests. . . ."

Such commands sometimes conflicted. Shortly after Hoess' father died, the World War broke out, and despite his mother's pleadings that he continue his studies, he lied about his age and managed to enlist at sixteen in the Twenty-first Regiment of Dragoons. He was sent to Turkey, then to the Iraqi front, then to Palestine. At eighteen he was already the commander of a cavalry unit. When the war ended, he refused to surrender and marched his own troops home through Turkey, Bulgaria, Romania, to Austria. He found his mother dead, his household dispersed. He took up arms again in one of the *Freikorps* units that fought in the Baltic states, and when the *Freikorps* became violently involved in the domestic battles of the Weimar Republic, Hoess too took part in an absurd political murder. He and a band of his comrades got drunk and then beat to death a schoolteacher whom they suspected of having informed on another nationalist. It was all a mistake. The schoolteacher had done nothing. Hoess was surprised to find himself arrested, prosecuted, and sentenced to life imprisonment.

By his own account, he was a model prisoner. "I had been taught since childhood to be absolutely obedient and meticulously tidy and clean," he wrote, "so in these matters I did not find it difficult to conform to the strict discipline of the prison." When the worthy liberals of Weimar devised a system in which meritorious prisoners might pass a series of tests and trials that would lead to their freedom, Hoess was proud to become the first of eight hundred prisoners to reach the top rating, and to wear three stripes on his sleeve. *Arbeit macht frei*. But as a political prisoner, he could not be freed. He began to go mad. He could not eat, could not get to sleep. "I had to . . . walk round and round my cell, and was unable to lie still," he wrote. "Then I would sink exhausted onto the bed and fall asleep, only to wake again after a short time bathed in sweat from my nightmares. In these confused dreams, I was always being pursued and killed, or falling over a precipice. Two hours of darkness became a torment. Night after night I heard the clocks strike the hour. As morning approached, my dread increased. I feared the light of day and the people I should have to see once more. . . ."

A prison doctor finally told Hoess that he was suffering from "prison psychosis," and that he would get over it, and he did. But it was not until 1928, when a left-right coalition came to power in Berlin, that an amnesty freed Hoess and an army of others who had committed political crimes. After five years in prison, Hoess passionately wanted to become a farmer. He discovered a right-wing group called the League of Artamanen, which was establishing a network of agricultural communes. He found a girl who shared his views, and they got married and worked the land and had three children (there were ultimately to be five). He learned in due time that one of the leaders of the Artamanen was Heinrich Himmler, scarcely thirty, a thoughtful young man who wore a pince-nez and loved birds and flowers and held a degree in agronomy and owned a chicken farm outside Munich. With the rise of Hitler, Himmler became the commander of the Führer's private guard, the Schutzstaffel, or SS, and when Himmler called for recruits, Hoess answered the call. He claims to have had "many doubts and hesitations" about leaving the farm, claims to have known almost nothing about the new concentration camps that Hitler was building. "To me it was just a question of being an active soldier again, or resuming my military career," Hoess wrote. "I went to Dachau."

Hoess' memoirs are full of lies and evasions, of course, but they also provide a remarkable illustration of the whole process of self-delusion. Having joined the SS for a quasi-military career, Hoess seems to have been surprised and strangely thrilled, at Dachau, the first time he saw a prisoner flogged. "When the man began to scream," he recalled, "I went hot and cold all over. . . . I am unable to give an explanation of this." Hoess dutifully regarded the prisoners as enemies of the state, regarded their forced labor as a justified punishment, regarded all the beatings and torments as a justified enforcement of discipline. He claims, nonetheless, to have had misgivings, and to have suppressed them. "I should have gone to [Himmler] and explained that I was not suited to concentration-camp service, because I felt too much sympathy for the prisoners. I was unable to find the courage to do this. . . . I did not wish to reveal my weakness. . . . I became reconciled to my lot."

Hoess worked hard, enforced orders, won promotions, first at Dachau, then at Sachsenhausen. Then came the war, and the lightning conquest of Poland. Himmler, who by now gloried in the title of *Reichsführer SS*, recognized Hoess' extraordinary dedication and ordered him to create the first concentration camp beyond the original frontiers of the Reich. Hoess sensed from the start that he was being assigned to a project of unprecedented dimensions. At the outbreak of the war, there had been six major concentration camps* in Germany, containing about 25,000 prisoners. Himmler told Hoess that he was to build, in the marshy valley of the Vistula, a camp for 10,000 prisoners, and that would be only the beginning. There might someday be 50,000 prisoners, or even more. "The numbers envisioned were at this time something entirely new in the history of concentration camps . . . " Hoess recalled. "Before the war the concentration camps had served the purposes of self-protection, but during the war, according to the will of the Reichsführer SS, they became a means to an end. They were now to serve the war effort, the munitions production. As many prisoners as possible were to become armaments workers. Every commandant had to run his camp ruthlessly with this end in view."

At Auschwitz, however, there was no camp, only a few

---

* The first was Dachau, just northwest of Munich, built in the spring of 1933, Hitler's first year. The others were Buchenwald, near Weimar; Sachsenhausen, north of Berlin; Mauthausen, near Linz; Flossenbürg, in the Sudetenland; and Ravensbrück, the women's prison, also north of Berlin. The SS rated these in three categories, with Dachau and Buchenwald being in Category I, the most lenient.

dilapidated barracks and stables. On May 20, 1940, a month after Hoess' arrival, an SS officer named Gerhard Pallitzsch, who held the title of *Rapportführer* and was responsible for camp discipline, brought to Hoess thirty German criminals whom he had selected from Sachsenhausen. To one of them, a man of Polish ancestry named Bruno Brodniewicz, belonged the sad distinction of being given the number one, the first of perhaps four million prisoners who were to be shipped to Auschwitz. These thirty German criminals were to start the building of the camp, and Pallitzsch had chosen them partly for their various technical skills. They were also destined to become the camp's first *Kapos,** or trusties, the men who upheld and carried out the orders of the SS and thus became not only the Nazis' representatives but in some cases the worst of oppressors.

The town council of Oswiecim, acting on behalf of a population of twelve thousand, cooperated. It ordered a roundup of two hundred local Jews and assigned them to start work on building the new camp. The SS office in Cracow sent fifteen cavalrymen to guard the prisoners as they worked. This work had barely begun when the police headquarters in Breslau sent a message to ask when the camp would be ready to take in prisoners. Before the message had even been answered, a passenger train arrived with 728 Polish political prisoners. The date was June 14, 1940. Most of these first pris-

---

* The origin of the word is unknown. According to one account, Italian workmen building roads in southern Germany used the Italian term for "head," *capo*, to address their foremen. Prisoners in the work gangs at Dachau overheard them and picked up their slang. From there, the word spread through all the concentration camps. Other accounts suggest that it may be a contraction of *Kamp Polizei* or *Kameradschafts Polizei*.

oners were young men who had been caught trying to escape
across the border into Hungary. There were also a few priests
and schoolteachers and Jews. They were assigned to some
buildings that belonged to the Polish Tobacco Monopoly and
were then ordered to join in building the camp.

Not many witnesses of those early days of Auschwitz
survived the long years of the war, and so the details remain
obscure, like the legends of the founding of some mythical
city. Hoess himself described the labors in terms of his own
dedication ("If I was to get the maximum effort out of my
officers and men, I had to set them a good example. When
reveille sounded for the SS men in the ranks, I too must get
out of bed. . . ."). Among the prisoners, however, Hoess'
guards applied from the beginning every technique that
would terrorize and subjugate their victims. The day began
with a roll call that often lasted for hours. The prisoners were
ordered to do their work on the run, and when they faltered
they were beaten with clubs. They sometimes had to line up
on their knees for their rations, a chunk of dark bread and a
bowl of watery soup. They were kicked and beaten at the
whim of any guard. If they complained or resisted, they were
beaten again, or simply shot.

On July 6, a prisoner named Tadeusz Wiejowski escaped.
Hoess ordered the other prisoners to stand at attention for a
roll call that lasted twenty hours. For three days, the SS men
hunted the fugitive but failed to find him. Hoess seized the
opportunity to order the expulsion of all Polish civilians from
seven peasant villages near Auschwitz. An area extending six
miles from north to south and almost three miles from west
to east was now decreed to be solely the property of the
Auschwitz prison camp.

More Polish prisoners kept streaming in. The first shipment from Warsaw arrived on August 15—513 political pris-

oners and 1,153 men caught in various roundups. Another shipment followed on September 21. The first snow fell in early October, and although the construction had been going on all summer, there had been little preparation for winter. Polish winters are hard. In that November of 1940, the temperature remained near zero. Icy mists rose from the Vistula every night and seeped through the unfinished barracks at Auschwitz. Many of these barracks had no windows. There was no heat. The prisoners had no winter clothes. Some worked barefoot in the snow.

When another captive escaped, Hoess decided to strengthen camp discipline by making all the other prisoners stand at roll call until 9 P.M. "From dawn heavy rain or sleet had been driving down and a strong northeast wind was blowing," one of the victims later recalled. "From noon onwards frozen men began to be carried or brought in on barrows ... half conscious, crawling, reeling like drunks, babbling incoherently and with difficulty, covered with spittle and foaming at the mouth, dying, gasping their last breath." And those were the early days, when Auschwitz was still being built, and served not as a death camp but just as a minor detention center for various categories of Polish prisoners.

In the midst of these difficulties, however, Hoess nourished grand plans to make Auschwitz a kind of Utopia. As early as January of 1941, while the prisoners were dying of cold, he decided to organize an Auschwitz symphony orchestra. Himmler, the former chicken farmer, indulged in similarly benign fantasies about his outpost on the Vistula. "Auschwitz was to become *the* agricultural research station for the eastern territories," Hoess recalled Himmler saying at a meeting in Berlin. "Opportunities were opened up to us, which we had never before had in Germany. Sufficient labor was available. All essential agricultural research must be carried out there. Huge laboratories and plant nurseries were to be set out. All kinds of stock-breeding was to be pursued there. . . ."

Sufficient labor was available. In that one sentence, that euphemism for the herds of emaciated prisoners in their tattered blue and white stripes, Hoess illuminated the most seductive element of Auschwitz in its first phase. It had been founded as a detention camp, a place to confine undesirable people, Polish army officers, dissidents and heretics of all sorts, people who must be prevented from infecting the new order that the Nazis were trying to build in the disorganized east. But once these thousands of people were stripped of their possessions and confined behind barbed wire, they represented a resource that Himmler was just beginning to appreciate: labor. That basic unit of human value was now available for any use to which the Reichsführer SS might choose to put it, whether an agricultural research laboratory or a symphony orchestra or an armaments factory. "In Auschwitz," said Hoess, "everything was possible."

Though the "sufficient labor" at Auschwitz could never really be sufficient to Himmler's fantasies, his primary imperative was to protect and enlarge this new resource. When he paid his first visit to the year-old outpost on the Vistula on March 1, 1941, he told Hoess that the camp he was building would contain not 10,000 or 50,000 prisoners, as previously agreed, but 100,000. In fact, Auschwitz itself was too small. A new camp, Auschwitz II, would have to be built in the birch woods outside what had once been the village of Brzezinka, two miles west of Auschwitz. The Germans called it Birkenau. This expansion was not mere SS imperialism, Himmler told Hoess, but a contribution to the war effort. He had brought with him several executives of I. G. Farben, the great chemical cartel, which was proposing to build a synthetic-rubber factory near Auschwitz in order to use the prisoners to make truck tires for the victorious Wehrmacht.

Hoess was appalled, not by the vastness of Himmler's plans but by the lack of means to carry them out. He had been officially warned in advance against reporting anything "disagreeable" to Himmler, but he could not prevent himself from an outpouring of bureaucratic protest. Auschwitz was already overcrowded by the trainloads of prisoners that kept rolling in, and there were no materials with which to build a new camp at Birkenau. The whole region lacked sufficient fresh water and drainage. There was a serious danger of disease. The local gauleiter joined in the protest, but Himmler was unmoved. The creation of Birkenau was an order. "Gentlemen, it will be built," said Himmler. "My reasons for constructing it are far more important than your objections. Ten thousand prisoners are to be provided for the I. G. Farben industries. . . ." As for the lack of building materials, the SS had now acquired its own brick and cement factories, which "will have to be made more productive." As for the lack of fresh water and drainage, Himmler dismissed these as "purely technical problems." In summation, he told Hoess, "I do not appreciate the difficulties in Auschwitz. It is up to you to manage somehow."

Hoess did manage. I. G. Farben began building its Buna synthetic-rubber factory in April in the nearby town of Dwory, and gangs of prisoners trudged there every morning to play their part in the war effort, but that summer changed the whole nature of the war, and therefore of the camp at Auschwitz. On the night of June 22, one of the prisoners heard on a clandestine radio that Hitler's panzer divisions were streaming across the Russian frontier. For a few days, the prisoners were jubilant, for they thought that the widened war and the new alliance among Hitler's enemies would inevitably lead to their liberation. But as the Wehrmacht swept across western Russia, the prisoners saw their future darken. Then came the first Russian captives, thousands and thousands of them. "They had been given hardly any food on the march," Hoess wrote, "during the halts on the way being simply turned out into the nearest fields and there told to 'graze' like cattle on anything edible they could find. In the Lamsdorf camp there must have been about 200,000 Russian prisoners of war. . . . Most of them huddled as best they could in earth hovels they had built themselves. . . . It was with these prisoners, many of whom could hardly stand, that I was now supposed to build the Birkenau prisoner-of-war camp."

It is not easy to compare the Nazis' treatment of different groups of prisoners, but the Russians seem to have received even more abuse than the Poles. Though both groups were regarded as subhuman *Untermenschen*, the Russians may have seemed more threatening, soldiers of a great power, now captives under the control of these uniformed Germans who had never been in combat. There was little thought of assigning the Russians to any project like the I. G. Farben plant; they were entirely expendable. Hoess ascribed the Russians' fate to their own weakness, or to a larger destiny. "They died like flies from general physical exhaustion," he recalled, "or from the most trifling maladies which their debilitated constitutions could no longer resist. I saw count-less Russians die while in the act of swallowing root vegetables or potatoes. . . . Overcome by the crudest instinct of self-preservation, they came to care nothing for one another, and in their selfishness now thought only of themselves. Cases of cannibalism were not rare in Birkenau. I myself came across a Russian lying between piles of bricks, whose body had been ripped open and the liver removed. They would beat each other to death for food. . . . They were no longer human beings."

Hoess seems to have persuaded himself that this process occurred all by itself, but one of his subordinates, Perry Broad, an SS man of Brazilian parentage, wrote out for the trial of twenty-two Auschwitz officials in Frankfurt in 1964 a vivid account of how the Russians were finally dispatched. "Thousands of prisoners of war were shot in a copse near Birkenau and buried in mass graves," Broad recalled. "The graves were about 150–200 feet long, 15 feet deep, and perhaps just as wide. The camp administration had solved the Russian problem to its satisfaction. Then . . . the fisheries began to complain that the fish in the ponds in the vicinity of Birkenau were dying. Experts said this was due to the pollution of the ground water through cadaveric poisoning. But that was not all. The summer sun was beating down on Birkenau, the bodies, which had not yet decomposed but had only rotted, started to swell up, and a dark red mass began to seep through the cracks of the earth, spreading an indescribable stench throughout. Something had to be done quickly. . . . SS Sergeant Franz Hössler was ordered to dig up the bodies in all possible secrecy and have them burned. . . ." Of the 12,000 Russians sent to build Birkenau in the fall of 1941, only about 150 were still alive the following summer. "Those who did remain were the best," said Hoess. "They were splendid workers."

*

While the authorities at Auschwitz were killing Russians, the authorities in Berlin were making new plans. In the summer of 1941—the exact date is unknown—Himmler summoned Hoess to Berlin for a secret meeting. Not even

Himmler's adjutant was present. "The Führer has ordered that the Jewish question be solved once and for all," Himmler said, according to Hoess, "and that we, the SS, are to implement that order." Himmler had considered using various camps in the east, he said, and only Auschwitz would serve as the center of destruction, only Auschwitz was sufficiently big, sufficiently isolated, sufficiently organized to carry out Himmler's plan. "I have now decided to entrust this task to you," Himmler said. "It is difficult and onerous and calls for complete devotion notwithstanding the difficulties that may arise. . . . You will treat this order as absolutely secret, even from your superiors. . . . The Jews are the sworn enemies of the German people and must be eradicated. Every Jew that we can lay our hands on is to be destroyed now during the war, without exception. . . ."

Hoess, the onetime pilgrim to Lourdes, seems by now to have reached such a state of official docility that he did not even question this incredible order, much less dispute it. The only question in his mind, apparently, was how such a gigantic enterprise could be carried out. Himmler did not explain. He said he would send Hoess an emissary, Major Adolf Eichmann, head of Section B-4 of Bureau IV of the Reich Security Office (RSHA), to discuss the details. Shortly afterward, Eichmann arrived in Auschwitz—a lean, wiry man with a sharp nose and a nervous manner. He and Hoess seemed to recognize something in each other that made them friends. Eichmann already had a plan, a geographic sequence for the shipment of Jews to Auschwitz, first those from the eastern part of Upper Silesia, then those from the neighboring Polish areas now under German rule, then those from Czechoslovakia, then a great sweep of Western Europe. . . .

But the two officials seemed unable to decide on the most fundamental question—how to kill the victims. The first bands of *Einsatzgruppen* who had prowled through Eastern Europe in the wake of the advancing German Army had simply shot any Jews they had found, but this was an inefficient way of carrying out mass executions. It was expensive. It was also bad for the morale of the executioners. This may seem a minor aspect of the problem, but the Germans gave it due weight. "It would have placed too heavy a burden on the SS men who had to carry it out," said Hoess, "especially because of the women and children among the victims."

Eichmann and Hoess agreed that poison gas was the solution, but the technology of gassing was only beginning to be explored. As early as 1939, the Nazis had started a series of experiments on the most feared and despised of all minorities, the mentally defective and the insane. In a dozen mental institutions in various parts of Germany, the Nazis built fake shower rooms into which they could pipe carbon-monoxide gas. Over the course of a year or more, they killed about fifty thousand mental patients in this way, but the technique was generally regarded as unsatisfactory. There were constant breakdowns in the gassing machinery, and the shower rooms could accommodate only about fifty victims at a time, and the disposal of the corpses caused unpleasant rumors in the surrounding towns.

There were also economic problems in applying such techniques on the grand scale envisaged at Auschwitz. Carbon-monoxide sprays "would necessitate too many buildings," as Hoess put it, "and it was also very doubtful whether the supply of gas for such a vast number of people would be available." The question was left open. Eichmann told Hoess that he would try to find a poisonous gas that was both cheap and plentiful, and then they would meet again. In the meantime, they strolled together through the idle farmlands that had been expropriated in the village of Brzezinka. They were

looking for a place where the gas, once it was found, might
be applied. They finally saw an abandoned farmhouse that
they considered, as Hoess said, "most suitable." It was near
the northern corner of the still-expanding camp. "It was isolated and screened by woods and hedges," Hoess wrote,
"and it was also not far from the railroad. The bodies could
be placed in the long deep pits in the nearby meadows. . . .
We calculated that after gasproofing the premises then available, it would be possible to kill about eight hundred people
simultaneously with a suitable gas."

The search for a suitable gas took Hoess to the other
death camps that were now being built.* To Chelmno, about
150 miles north of Auschwitz, where the inhabitants of the
Lodz ghetto were herded into a crumbling château known as
"the palace," then loaded onto trucks that had been specially
equipped so that the exhaust fumes could be piped up into
the rear compartment. By the time the trucks arrived at a burial ground in the surrounding forest, the prisoners in the back
were dead. This system had its flaws, however. The trucks
could not handle large numbers of prisoners, and the gas
from the exhaust pipes flowed in so unevenly that some of
the victims were still gasping with life when the trucks
reached the burial ground. Hoess moved on to Treblinka,
near Byalystok, where the plan was to park the trucks filled
with prisoners outside three small gas chambers, each about
fifteen feet square, and to pipe the exhaust fumes in among
the prisoners assembled there. Hoess was still dissatisfied.

---

* Auschwitz was by far the biggest of the death camps, but there were five
others, all in Poland, put into operation between December of 1941 and the
middle of 1942. They were: Chelmno (Kulmhof), Belzec, Sobibor, Majdanek,
and Treblinka.

All these methods were too unreliable, too small in scale.

Hoess apparently was not aware, nor was Eichmann, that the suitable gas was already available. It was called Zyklon B,* a commercial form of hydrocyanic acid, which became active on contact with air. It was manufactured by a firm called Degesch, which was largely owned by I. G. Farben, and it had been brought to Auschwitz in the summer of 1941 as a vermin-killer and disinfectant. It was very dangerous. Two civilians came from Hamburg with their gas masks to show the Auschwitz authorities how to use the poison. Prisoners who worked in the munitions plant had to hang up their vermin-infested clothes, and then the barracks were sealed, and the gas was released.

One of the judges who presided at the 1964 Auschwitz trial in Frankfurt wanted to know exactly how the gas worked. "Was it granular?" he asked.

"Zyklon B was packed in small, two-pound containers which at first resembled cardboard disks, something like beer coasters, always a bit damp and gray," said one of the defendants, Arthur Breitweiser, who had worked in the Auschwitz administrative office. He told how the gas containers had to be pried open with a hammer. "Then we went into the rooms and scattered the stuff . . ." Breitweiser said. "Zyklon B worked terribly fast. I remember one of the SS men going into a house that had already been disinfected. The ground floor had been aired out in the evening, and the next morning the man wanted to open the windows on the first floor. He must have inhaled some fumes, because he collapsed immediately and rolled down the steps, unconscious, out into the fresh air.

---

* The term comes from the first letters of the German names for the three main ingredients, cyanide, chlorine and nitrogen.

Had he fallen the other way, he wouldn't have lived."

On September 3, 1941, while Hoess was away on business, Deputy Commandant Karl Fritzsch decided, apparently
on his own authority, to experiment in using Zyklon B on 600
Russian prisoners of war and 250 tubercular patients in the
Auschwitz hospital. He sealed up some of the underground
bunkers of Block 11, headquarters of the Gestapo's Politische
Abteilung, or Political Department. There he packed in the
prisoners, then put on a gas mask and flung one of the disinfectant containers into the midst of the victims. Within a few
minutes, they were all dead. "Those who were propped
against the door leaned with a curious stiffness and then fell
right at our feet, striking their faces hard against the concrete
floor," recalled a Pole named Zenon Rozanski, who served in
the penal detail assigned to clear out the bunker. "Corpses!
Corpses standing bolt upright and filling the entire corridor
of the bunker, till they were packed so tight it was impossible
for more to fall."

Almost by accident, Captain Fritzsch had discovered the
technology that Hoess and Eichmann were seeking, a technology that was "suitable." And Birkenau, where the giant
crematoria were to arise, had not yet even been built. It was
not until October 15, 1941, that Hoess approved a plan
designed by one of the prisoners in the Auschwitz Building
Office. To house 100,000 prisoners, as Himmler had ordered,
the plan called for a series of two-story barracks to be built in
a rectangle 400 feet in width by 2,300 feet in length. Each barracks was to contain three tiers of bunks, with four to six prisoners in each bunk. No sooner had the building been started
than Hans Kammler, an engineer in the SS administrative
headquarters in Berlin, arrived in Auschwitz with the news
that Birkenau was to house not 100,000 prisoners but 200,000.

The Final Solution lurched into existence. It was perfectly

clear in Himmler's meeting with Hoess in the summer of 1941, but there were endless details to be worked out, regulations to be drafted and distributed, meetings and elaborations. The most important of these was the secret Wannsee Conference convened by Himmler's alter ego, Reinhard Heydrich, at a villa in the beautiful lakeside suburb on the southwestern edge of Berlin. It was originally scheduled for December 9, 1941, but the Japanese attack on Pearl Harbor caused a certain amount of confusion, and so the conference was rescheduled for January 20, 1942. Lunch and drinks were served. There were thirteen officials representing the Foreign Office, the Ministry of Justice, the Polish occupation authorities, all the main departments of the German government and the Nazi Party. Heydrich spoke at length of "the coming Final Solution of the Jewish question." Everything was explained. Eichmann kept the minutes.

Yet there were still further delays. It was not until August 3, 1942, that the working plans for the four great crematoria, which could take in as many as ten thousand prisoners per day, were approved by the Auschwitz authorities and the engineers at Toepf A. G. in Erfurt. In January and February of 1943, there were still complaints of work delayed by freezing weather, and only on March 13 was Crematorium II finally ready to operate. Until then, as Himmler had ordered, it was up to Hoess "to manage somehow." Hoess managed with the farmhouse that he and Eichmann had discovered. There and in an abandoned barn about three hundred prisoners a day could be gassed. Hundreds more were killed by lethal injections of phenol, or by simple shooting. Throughout the confusions of 1942, the impossible orders kept pouring in, and Hoess kept improvising. "I cannot say," he wrote in his memoir, "on what date the extermination of the Jews began . . . "

The first *Transport Juden*, consisting of 999 Jewish women

from Slovakia, arrived on March 26, 1942, at the Auschwitz
railroad station. "A cheerful little station," as a prisoner
named Tadeusz Borowski later wrote, "very much like any
other provincial railway stop: a small square framed by tall
chestnuts and paved with yellow gravel. . . ." Since the
Birkenau gas chambers had not yet been built, the women
were stripped, their heads shaved, and then they were confined in Blocks 1 to 10 of the main camp, separated by a high
fence from the men's barracks. Then they were made to stand
for hours at roll call, and beaten, and then sent out in work
gangs, and beaten again.

And at the little station lined with chestnut trees, the
trains kept arriving. On April 17, 1942, another shipment of
973 Slovakian Jews appeared at Auschwitz, and on April 19,
another 464. The SS men and their snarling guard dogs met
them at the railroad ramp. Prisoner Borowski, who had been
a poet of incandescent talent,* appeared at the ramp occasionally to watch the arrivals. "The ramp has become increasingly alive with activity, increasingly noisy," he later wrote of
one such scene. "The crews are being divided into those who
will open and unload the arriving cattle cars and those who
will be posted by the wooden steps. . . . Motorcycles drive up,
delivering SS officers, bemedaled, glittering with brass, beefy
men with highly polished boots and shiny, brutal faces. Some
have brought their briefcases, others hold thin, flexible
whips. . . . Some stroll majestically on the ramp, the silver
squares on their collars glitter, the gravel crunches under
their boots, their bamboo whips snap impatiently. . . . The

---

* Borowski survived three years in Auschwitz, published three collections
of stories and a volume of poetry after the war. He committed suicide in
1951 at the age of twenty-nine.

train rolls slowly alongside the ramp. In the tiny barred windows appear pale, wilted, exhausted human faces, terror-stricken women with tangled hair, unshaven men. They gaze at the station in silence. And then, suddenly, there is a stir inside the cars, and a pounding against the wooden boards. 'Water! Air!'"

The SS men routed the starving and terrified prisoners out of the freight cars, ordered them to abandon all their possessions, and then whipped them into line to prepare for the process known as "selection." Two SS doctors had been assigned by rotation to choose a few of the hardiest prisoners to be preserved for the Auschwitz labor *Kommandos*. These doctors—the most notable was Josef Mengele, who liked to wear white gloves and to whistle themes from Wagner's operas as he worked—surveyed each newcomer for a few seconds and then waved him on in one direction or another. A wave to the right meant—though most of the newcomers did not realize it—survival, an assignment to hard labor in the construction gangs. A wave to the left meant the gas chamber. Anyone more than about forty years of age was waved to the left. Most women went to the left. Almost all children under fifteen went to the left. Families that asked to stay together were reunited and sent to the left. Only about ten percent of each transport, on the average, went to the right. Sometimes more, sometimes less, according to the whim of the SS doctors.

The May 12 transport that brought 1,500 Jews from Sosnowiec marked a turning point in the short history of Auschwitz, for this was the first trainload of Jews who were not imprisoned, not shorn, not sent out in work gangs, not beaten or shot. This time, there was no selection on the ramp at the railroad station, no division of families, no separation of those who were fit to work from the old and the sick and the children. These 1,500 Jews from Sosnowiec were the first to be sent directly to the gas chamber, all of them. And with that, Auschwitz finally became what it had always been destined to become, not just a prisoner-of-war camp, not just a slave-labor camp, but a *Vernichtungslager*, an extermination camp. *Vernichtung* means more than that. It means to make something into nothing. Annihilation.

*

That summer of 1942, the trains to Auschwitz began bringing the Jews from France, Belgium and Holland. Also the Jews from Croatia. In November came the Jews of Norway. In March of 1943, when the great crematoria finally began operating, came the first of the Jews of Greece, from Macedonia and Thrace. That same spring, after the destruction of the rebellious Warsaw ghetto, the SS began the systematic liquidation of all the remaining Polish ghettos. Lwow was one of the first, then Byalystok. In September, the ghettos of Minsk and Vilna were destroyed. In October, Auschwitz received the Jews of southern France and Rome, in December the Jews of northern Italy, then, early in 1944, the Jews of Athens . . .

"What for Hitler . . . was among the war's main objectives . . . and what for Eichmann was a job . . . " Hannah Arendt wrote in *Eichmann in Jerusalem*, "was for the Jews quite literally the end of the world."

*

Despite the annihilation of the 1,500 Jews from Sosnowiec, the selections on the ramp continued, for there was never a consistent policy on anything at Auschwitz, not even on killing. The basic orders from Berlin were completely contradictory. Eichmann and his cohorts at police headquarters, the RSHA, continually demanded more killings, but the SS economic offices, the WVHA, demanded just as adamantly that the prisoners be made to work for the war effort. So the Auschwitz authorities carried out their orders, murdering or sparing their victims, by a strange mixture of bureaucracy and impulse. "We were all tormented by secret doubts," said Hoess, "[but] I myself dared not admit to such doubts. . . . Often at night, I would walk through the stables and seek relief among my beloved animals."

In the midst of all the killing, according to Ella Lingens, a Viennese doctor who was sent to Auschwitz in 1943 for helping Jews to escape from Austria, there remained one place that Dr. Lingens called an "island of peace," the Babice labor camp. "That was the work of one man alone," Dr. Lingens testified at the Frankfurt trial in 1964. His name was Flacke. "How he did it, I don't know. His camp was clean, and the food also. The women called him 'Daddy,' and he even got eggs from outside. . . . I don't know what happened to him. I once talked to him. 'You know, sir,' I said. 'Everything we do is so horrible, so pointless. Because when this war ends we'll all be murdered. No witnesses will be allowed to survive.' And Flacke answered, 'I hope there will be enough among us to prevent that.'"

The Frankfurt judge, who had heard endless protestations about irresistible orders from higher authorities, was amazed by Dr. Lingens' testimony. "Do you wish to say," he asked, "that everyone could decide for himself to be either good or evil in Auschwitz?"

"That is exactly what I wish to say," Dr. Lingens answered.

The Auschwitz hospital illustrates the central paradox. In theory, there was no reason why a death camp should have a hospital at all, and yet the one at Auschwitz grew to considerable size, with about sixty doctors and more than three hundred nurses. It had a surgical department and an operating theater, and special sections for infectious diseases, internal injuries and dentistry. Yet the lord of this domain was Dr. Mengele, the chief physician at Birkenau, who labored long hours on testing and then killing captive twins in a futile effort to find new ways of increasing the German birth rate. Olga Lengyel, the wife of a Romanian psychiatrist, served as a prisoner-nurse in Auschwitz and recalled after the war that Mengele once insisted on personally delivering the baby of a pregnant prisoner. "I saw him take every precaution during the accouchement," she wrote, "watching to see that all aseptic principles were rigorously observed and that the umbilical cord was cut with care. Half an hour later he sent the mother and child to the crematory oven."

The hospital facilities for prisoners were extremely primitive at first, operated by the prisoners themselves and lacking even basic medicines, but the Nazis soon realized that the prisoners' diseases were a danger to their guardians as well. The worst of these was typhus, which invaded the camp with a shipment of prisoners from Lublin in April of 1941. The Nazis' favored remedy was to gas anyone who came to the hospital for treatment. The result was that stricken prisoners avoided the hospital, and so, by the summer of 1942, typhus had become epidemic, killing as many as three hundred prisoners a day. The SS authorities, feeling threatened themselves, could not decide what to do. They periodically wandered through the wards of the hospital, checking the patients' records and making their own diagnoses. Many of those whom they judged unfit were dragged off to the gas chambers. Others were subjected to a lethal injection of phenol, directly into the heart.

Yet although thousands were murdered in the Auschwitz hospital, thousands more were saved. It became, in fact, one of the camp's chief sanctuaries. Its staff, headed by a German homosexual criminal named Hans Bock, was infiltrated and even dominated by the Polish underground that had begun to organize resistance in Auschwitz. And just as the SS doctors had the right to murder anyone, they also had the right to forbid the Gestapo to seize their patients. "I know of almost no SS man who could not claim to have saved someone's life," Dr. Lingens testified in an attempt to explain the myriad contradictions of Auschwitz. "There were few sadists. Not more than five or ten percent were pathological criminals in the clinical sense. The others were all perfectly normal men who knew the difference between right and wrong. They all knew what was going on."

No less paradoxical was the system of justice at Auschwitz. In principle, there was no system except that of force, no rule that could not be broken. The SS men and the *Kapos* who served them could beat or torment or murder the prisoners for any reason they chose, or for no reason at all. And so it was up to the prisoners themselves to institute a crude form of justice, crude and inadequate, but nonetheless justice. Though much of camp life was based on the principle of survival, kangaroo courts met at night. A prisoner accused of stealing another prisoner's food could be sentenced to twenty-five lashes; an informer could be sentenced to death.

And then there appeared, in the middle of 1943, the implausible figure of Dr. Konrad Morgen, an SS judge assigned to investigate the corruption that infested the concentration camps. The incoming prisoners had been stripped of all their possessions—even their shorn hair was destined to make pillows—and everything of value was supposed to be sent to SS headquarters in Berlin. In actual fact, it was stored, piled up to the ceilings, in a row of thirty barracks known as "Canada,"* and Canada soon became the largest black market in Europe. Everything that accumulated there could be "organized," as the Auschwitz slang called it, meaning stolen, sold, traded. Canada had everything, not just the basic supplies of food and clothing but diamonds, tapestries, silk underwear, the finest cognac. In the last days of Auschwitz, in January of 1945, the SS men who were evacuating the camp set Canada afire and burned all but six of its thirty barracks, but even in that charred ruin the Russians found an almost incredible quantity of things that had once belonged to the dead: 836,255 women's outfits, 38,000 pairs of men's shoes, 13,964 carpets . . .

Judge Morgen, assigned to the absurd task of imposing law on the lawless SS, proved to be a fanatic about carrying out his mission. His first inquiries into corruption had been so diligent that his superiors had shipped him off to fight on the Russian front, but then other officials had maneuvered to bring him back. Morgen personally investigated the financial operations of Karl Koch, commandant at Buchenwald, and had Koch arrested, prosecuted and executed. What brought him to Auschwitz was an intercepted packet of gold that an SS man there had sent home to his wife. Morgen wandered into one of the crematoria and was startled to find half-drunk SS men lolling about in a lounge and being served potato pancakes by attractive female prisoners. "They were being waited on like pashas," he later testified at the Frankfurt trial.

---

* The Polish prisoners originally gave it this name because it evoked that land of legendary wealth to which many of their relatives had emigrated before the war.

Although Morgen was supposed to limit himself to the question of corruption, he returned to Berlin and filed a murder charge against the chief Gestapo officer at Auschwitz, Lieutenant Maximilian Grabner. Such a move naturally amazed the police bureaucracy, but if an SS judge filed a murder charge, then the bureaucracy had to deal with it. Grabner was thereupon removed from his post at Auschwitz and brought back to Berlin for questioning about all the killings in Block 11, about the corruption in Canada, and even about the affair he was having with a woman prisoner. He was eventually sentenced to twelve years in prison (and later retried and executed by the Poles). Morgen survived everything and resumed the practice of law in postwar Germany.

"Do you wish to say that everyone could decide for himself to be either good or evil in Auschwitz?"

"That is exactly what I wish to say."

*

SS Sergeant Josef Schillinger was a short, stocky man with light blond hair and bright blue eyes. A stern disciplinarian, he liked to make surprise inspections and to punish the prisoners for the slightest infraction of camp rules. He liked to stand at the entrance to the gas chambers and watch as the prisoners filed in. He also liked to appear at the railroad ramp and watch the arriving prisoners being divided, assigned to the work gangs or to the gas chambers.

On October 23, 1943, Sergeant Schillinger was marching up and down this ramp, pistol in hand, when he spotted an attractive Jewish woman who had just arrived in one of the cattle cars. When she saw that he was watching her, she provocatively returned his look. Sergeant Schillinger reached out and seized her by the arm. The woman twisted away, reached down and threw a handful of gravel into his face. Schillinger raised his arms to protect himself, and that made

him drop his pistol. The woman pounced on it. Then she shot
Sergeant Schillinger in the abdomen, several times. Other SS
men soon tore the gun away from her and clubbed her onto
the truck bound for the gas chamber. Sergeant Schillinger lay
face down on the ramp, dying, his fingers clawing in the
gravel. *"O Gott, mein Gott,"* he groaned, *"was hab' ich getan,
das ich so leiden muss?"* Which means "Oh God, my God, what
have I done that I must suffer so?"

   "That," said Dr. Lingens, *"is exactly what I wish to say."*

*

   This Auschwitz that arose out of the swamps and waste-
lands on the Vistula ultimately grew to a prison empire of
nearly 150,000 inhabitants. Out of nothing, Hoess built a city
comparable in size to Tangier or Aberdeen or Cedar Rapids,
Iowa. But its importance was that it represented a microcosm
of Nazi Europe, and thus a microcosm of what twentieth-
century Europe itself had become. The civilized world that
had once been ruled from Rome was now ruled from Berlin,
and the principles of that Nazi civilization were the govern-
ing principles of Auschwitz.

   These principles sometimes seemed to involve nothing
more than the ceaseless conflict between the lust for destruction and the lust for survival, and yet Auschwitz was a society
of extraordinary complexity. It had its own soccer stadium,
its own library, its own photographic lab, and its own symphony orchestra. It had its own Polish nationalist underground and its own Polish Communist underground—not to
mention separate Russian, Slovakian, French and Austrian
resistance groups—whose members fought and sometimes
killed one another. It also had its underground religious services, Catholic, Protestant and Jewish alike. Auschwitz even
had its own brothel, known as "the puff," which favored
prisoners could enter by earning chits for good behavior.

Crafty veterans of the camp would gather at the office where the chits were handed out, and if any model prisoner failed to claim his due, one of the old-timers would quickly step forward to claim it for him.

"Concentration-camp existence . . . taught us that the whole world is really like a concentration camp," wrote Tadeusz Borowski. "The weak work for the strong, and if they have no strength or will to work—then let them steal, or let them die. . . . There is no crime that a man will not commit in order to save himself. And, having saved himself, he will commit crimes for increasingly trivial reasons; he will commit them first out of duty, then from habit, and finally—for pleasure. . . . The world is ruled by neither justice nor morality; crime is not punished nor virtue rewarded, one is forgotten as quickly as the other. The world is ruled by power. . . ."

This Hobbesian/Brechtian creed is not true. Most of those who survived Auschwitz did so because of a powerful faith in something outside themselves—family, friendship, patriotism, religion—and nobody survived without help. Those who lived alone died alone. Undeniably, the doctrine of survival-at-all-costs was what the Nazis had decreed when they first rounded up the Jews of the occupied territories into a series of ghettos, but even when the victims huddled in their new captivity, they could still hope for some kind of reprieve. "The barbed wire which fenced us in did not cause us any real fear," Elie Wiesel wrote of his native town in *Night*. "We even thought ourselves rather well off; we were entirely self-contained. A little Jewish republic." For every warning of impending deportations, there was some rumor of explanation. Why would the Germans waste military resources in deporting people to the east? Besides, how long could the war last? When the deportation orders finally came, the victims yearned to believe the official announcements about resettlement colonies in the east. "The women were cooking eggs," Wiesel wrote of the last day before the departure to Auschwitz, "roasting meat, baking cakes and making knapsacks. The children wandered all over . . . "

The trip to Auschwitz served as a kind of initiation. The Nazis crowded the victims into freight cars, usually about one hundred people to each car, and then locked them in. There was no food or water, no toilet, no air. Those who had brought a few sandwiches or pieces of fruit soon found themselves fighting to defend their treasures. When their supplies were gone, there was nothing. Children cried endlessly. The old weakened and died. Corpses lay where they fell, among the battered suitcases held together with rope.

The freight cars came from as far as Bordeaux and Rome and Salonika, voyages of a week or more, stifling in summer, arctic in winter. Sometimes the trains were shunted onto sidings for days on end, nights on end. The prisoners' cries for water went unheeded. When they banged their fists on the doors, their guards usually ignored them. Occasionally, they answered by banging the outsides of the doors with their gun butts. Sometimes, by the time the sealed trains finally reached southern Poland, the dead outnumbered the living. (The trip from Corfu took twenty-seven days, and when the train came to a stop, no survivors emerged at all.) To arrive at the unknown town of Auschwitz, then, seemed a kind of liberation.

"A huge, multicolored wave of people loaded down with luggage pours from the train," Borowski continued his description of the scene on the ramp, "like a blind, mad river trying to find a new bed. But before they have a chance to recover, before they can draw a breath of fresh air and look at the sky, bundles are snatched from their hands, coats ripped off their backs, their purses and umbrellas taken away. . . .

"*Verboten!*" one of us barks through clenched teeth. There is an SS man standing behind your back, calm, efficient, watchful. 'Meine Herrschaften, this way, ladies and gentlemen, try not to throw your things around, please. . . .'"

Such courtliness occasionally suited the SS sense of humor, but the Nazis had whips and used them freely. The arrival on the ramp was usually a chaos of screams and shouts, barking guard dogs, pandemonium. The *Begrüssung* (welcome), the Nazis called it. When the train was emptied, a thin, pockmarked SS man ordered Borowski and his fellow prisoners to clean out the debris. "In the corners," Borowski wrote, "amid human excrement and abandoned wristwatches, lie squashed, trampled infants, naked little monsters with enormous heads and bloated bellies."

Once the prisoners were assembled on the ramp, the two SS doctors made their selection, a wave here, a gesture there. While those on the right remained standing on the ramp, the rest, including most of the women and children, were pushed onto trucks and driven off. One of the trucks was reassuringly marked with a large red cross. That was the one that carried the sealed canisters of Zyklon B. When the newcomers arrived at their destination, officially known as Bunker No. 1, they saw two neat little farmhouses, with thatched roofs and whitewashed walls, surrounded by fruit trees and shrubbery. Teams of Jewish prisoners who had been assigned to the *Sonderkommando*, or special command, shepherded the victims onward, urging them to move along quietly into the shower rooms and to take off all their clothes. Some of them may have guessed what lay ahead. Most of them, in a state of terror, shock and exhaustion, simply did as they were told. They had heard that terrible things would happen to them in the resettlement camps of the east, but so many terrible things had already happened in the railroad cars and on the ramp that they found it hard to imagine anything worse to come. Few of them noticed, as they crowded naked in the shower room, that although there were water pipes and sprays along the ceiling, there were no water drains in the floor.

Here, and later in the four new crematoria at Birkenau, the Final Solution took place. What happened can best be described in the detached tones of Rudolf Hoess, who was in command of all this: "The door would now be quickly screwed up and the gas discharged by the waiting disinfectors through vents in the ceilings of the gas chambers, down a shaft that led to the floor. This insured the rapid distribution of the gas. It could be observed through the peephole in the door that those who were standing nearest to the induction vents were killed at once. It can be said that about one third died straightaway. The remainder staggered about and began to scream and struggle for air. The screaming, however, soon changed to the death rattle and in a few minutes all lay still. . . . The door was opened half an hour after the induction of the gas, and the ventilation switched on. . . . The special detachment now set about removing the gold teeth and cutting the hair from the women. After this, the bodies were taken up by elevator and laid in front of the ovens, which had meanwhile been stoked up. Depending on the size of the bodies, up to three corpses could be put into one oven at the same time. The time required for cremation . . . took twenty minutes."

There were some prisoners who cherished the idea that Hoess had somehow exceeded his orders and begun these massacres on his own authority, and that if the authorities in Berlin knew what was really happening, they would stop it. Such speculations ended with Heinrich Himmler's second visit to Auschwitz in July of 1942. He stayed for two days and inspected everything. He started, according to Hoess' account, with the more benign parts of the camp, "the agri-cultural areas, the building of the dam, the laboratories and plant-breeding establishments, . . . the stock-breeding centers and the tree nurseries." Then he "watched the whole process of destruction of a transport of Jews, which had just arrived." He started by watching the selections on the railroad ramp, then watched the victims being taken to the gas chambers, then watched them die. He could smell the awful smell of burning flesh, which lingered in the air after the cremations. "He made no remark regarding the process of extermina-tion," Hoess recalled, "but remained quite silent."

Hoess repeatedly complained of his difficulties, pointing out the overcrowding and the shortages, the emaciation and illness among the prisoners. "I want to hear no more about difficulties," Himmler finally snapped at him. "An SS officer does not recognize difficulties." That evening, the Reichsführer SS was "extremely amiable" at a dinner for his officers and their wives. "He discussed the education of children and new buildings and books and pictures," Hoess reported. The next night, shortly before departing, Himmler told Hoess, "I have seen your work and the results you have achieved, and I am satisfied and thank you for your services."

The following January, 1943, Himmler paid a third visit to inspect the progress of the Final Solution. He arrived at Auschwitz at 8 A.M., and by 8:45 one of the gas chambers was packed with victims so that the Reichsführer SS could watch a gassing at 9 o'clock sharp. At 8:55, however, a telephone rang, and the executioners learned that Himmler and Hoess were still having breakfast. "Inside the chamber itself," according to the recollections of a Czech prisoner named Rudolf Vrba, "frantic men and women, who knew by that time what a shower in Auschwitz meant, began shouting, screaming, and pounding weakly on the door. . . . " Nobody paid any attention. The SS men waited for orders. At 10 A.M., they were told to wait some more. At 11 A.M., an official car finally arrived, bringing Himmler and Hoess, who paused to chat with the senior officers present. Hoess invited Himmler to observe through a peephole the naked mass sealed inside the gas chamber. Himmler obliged. Then the gassing began. "Hoess courteously invited his guest to have another peep through the observation window," Vrba recalled. "For some minutes, Himmler peered into the death chamber, obviously impressed. . . . What he had seen seemed to have satisfied him and put him in good humor. Though he rarely smoked, he accepted a cigarette from an officer, and, as he puffed at it rather clumsily, he laughed and joked."

*

Those happy few who survived the selections on the ramp were marched off to the quarantine barracks, where they were initiated into a series of rituals designed to destroy their identity and their personality and thus their capacity for resistance. First they were taken to the yard between Blocks 15 and 16 and ordered to strip off all their clothes. All their hair was shaved off. Then they had to run to a nearby bath-house and take a cold shower. Then they had to run to another yard where they were provided with ill-fitting blue-and-white striped prison uniforms and wooden clogs. Their uniforms bore triangles of different colors, according to the categories of prisoners—green for professional criminals, red for political opposition, black for prostitutes and other "aso-cials," pink for homosexuals, purple for fundamentalist "exponents of the Bible." (Jews who fitted any of these categories had their yellow triangle superimposed on the other triangle to form a Star of David.) Finally, the prisoners were tattooed on the left forearm with their prison number.

Henceforth, they were told, they were to be known only by this number, not by name. This whole procedure normally took all day, but if the prisoners had arrived in the afternoon, it took all night. Throughout it, they were given no food or water. "For the first time," said Primo Levi, an Italian chemist who arrived in bewilderment at this northern hell, "we became aware that our language lacks words to express this offense: the demolition of a man. . . . We had reached the bottom. It is not possible to sink lower than this; no human condition is more miserable than this, nor could it conceivably be so. Nothing belongs to us any more; they have taken away our clothes, our shoes, even our hair; if we speak, they will not listen to us, and if they listen, they will not understand. They will even take away our name. . . ." All too soon, Levi learned that this "bottom" was only a way station on the road to still lower levels of degradation.

Just as the arrival in Auschwitz seemed a relief after days in the crowded freight cars, the arrival in the quarantine barracks seemed a relief after the process of selection and registration. It was, however, a new kind of ordeal, designed to test whether the SS doctors on the ramp had been correct in their choice of survivors. Roll call was at 4:30 A.M., and sometimes the prisoners had to stand there all day long. They were drilled in camp routine, trained to form ranks of five and to take off their caps on command, to perform such drudgery as digging ditches and moving rocks, and to take part in "physical training." This physical training, also known as "sport," consisted of running in position until a *Kapo* ordered the prisoners to drop to the ground and start hopping like frogs, until a *Kapo* ordered the prisoners to get up and start running again. "Sport" is a fairly common form of gymnastic drill, but the Auschwitz version lasted for hours, and anyone who fal-

tered was kicked and beaten. After a fifteen-minute break for
lunch, the SS training continued with, for example, singing
classes. Jews were taught to chorus an anti-Semitic song
called *"O Du mein Jerusalem"*; prisoners of all kinds were
taught a song in praise of their own imprisonment, *"Im Lager
Auschwitz war Ich zwar so manchen Monaten . . .* (In Camp
Auschwitz I have spent so many months . . .)" At 3 P.M., the
"sport" resumed, until 6:30. Then came another roll call,
sometimes two hours long. Those who failed to satisfy their
guards had to stand at attention all night. Lagerführer
Fritzsch, the man who had first tried out Zyklon B on the
Russian prisoners, liked to tell the newcomers, "You have
come to a concentration camp, not to a sanatorium, and there
is only one way out—through the chimney. Anyone who
does not like it can try hanging himself on the wires.* If there
are Jews in this draft, they have no right to live longer than a
fortnight; if there are priests, their period is one month—the
rest, three months."

After four to eight weeks in quarantine, the prisoners
came to believe that life might be better if they could only
reach the main camp. Once again, they were deluded.
Auschwitz was designed, just as Fritzsch warned, to work
its victims to death. More than one thousand prisoners were
herded into brick barracks built for four hundred. They
slept in three-tiered wooden bunks, half a dozen men to a
bunk, often with no mattresses or blankets. There was little

---

* An Auschwitz slang phrase that described the most easily available form of
suicide. Anyone who ran toward the electrified wire fence that surrounded the
camp was instantly fired on by SS men in the watch towers. If he succeeded in
reaching the wire fence, he was immediately electrocuted by 6,000 volts.

heat and less ventilation. The place stank. The prisoners' only consolation was that Birkenau was even worse. Instead of overcrowded brick barracks, there were overcrowded wooden huts, with leaking roofs and dirt floors that turned to mud. Auschwitz had yellowish running water and a primitive sewage system; Birkenau had only a few privies. At least half of the prisoners—and often two thirds or more—suffered the miseries and humiliations of chronic diarrhea. At night, the only facilities were a few overflowing buckets. And the rats were everywhere. When someone died during the night, according to a prisoner named Judith Sternberg Newman, the rats "would get at the body before it was cold, and eat the flesh in such a way that it was unrecognizable before morning."

In both camps, the first ordeal of the day was, as always, the *Appell*, or roll call, which began at about 4:30 A.M., somewhat before dawn, rain or shine, or frost or snow. Everyone had to stand in line, in rows of five, while the counting began. No exceptions or excuses were permitted. The sick were dragged from their bunks to take part. Even those who had died during the night were carried out and propped up in position so that they could be counted. As the dawn brightened, the *Kapo*s sauntered up and down the ranks of the prisoners, counting, and hitting anyone they felt like hitting. Sometimes they insisted that the shortest prisoners fill the ranks at the front; sometimes the positions were reversed, with the shortest prisoners in the back. Anyone who didn't move quickly enough was clubbed. And there were always the dogs, snarling and straining at their leashes. At any interruption or disturbance, any break or error in the counting, the process began all over again. The roll call generally lasted three or four hours—punitive roll calls lasted much longer—and only at about eight o'clock did the SS officers arrive to review the roll-call numbers and send the prisoners out to work.

Arbeit macht frei. The prisoners marched off to the booming accompaniment of the Auschwitz band,* but without food, or only with the food they had saved from the previous night's ration, or bought or bartered or stolen during the night. Officially, the prisoners were given just enough food to survive. The rations provided for a breakfast of one-half liter of grain coffee or herb tea. The main meal at noon theoretically consisted of one liter of meat soup four times a week and vegetable soup three times a week. The ingredients were carefully listed in the regulations: The meat soup was supposed to contain 150 grams of potatoes, 150 grams of cabbage, kale or beetroot, 20 grams of meat. At night, the ration was 350 grams of black bread, sometimes with a sliver of margarine or a dab of beet-sugar jam. In fact, the prisoners never got more than a fraction of their rations. The authorities who bought the supplies regularly saved money by acquiring rotten meat and spoiled vegetables. The guards and the cooks took the best share for themselves, to eat or to trade. What the prisoners actually received was a bread made partly of sawdust and a soup made of thistles, or worse. Sometimes, according to Olga Lengyel, it was simply called "surprise soup" because it contained such unexpected ingredients as buttons, keys, tufts of hair, dead mice and, on one occasion, a small metal sewing kit complete with needles and thread.

---

* There is a widespread legend that the SS had Schubert and Beethoven performed while they managed the Holocaust, but the talents of the Auschwitz band hardly exceeded what was necessary for a few popular tunes and marches, endlessly repeated.

Awful as the food was, the prisoners fought over their shares, and even over the crude bowls from which to eat. Among the 1,500 women in Mrs. Lengyel's barracks, the Nazis distributed just twenty bowls, each containing about two liters, and one pail. "The barracks chief . . . immediately commandeered the pail as a chamber pot," Mrs. Lengyel recalled. "Her cronies quickly snatched the other bowls for the same use. What could the rest of us do? It seemed as though the Germans constantly sought to pit us against each other, to make us competitive, spiteful, and hateful. In the morning, we had to be content with rinsing the bowls as well as we could before we put in our minute rations. . . . The first days our stomachs rose at the thought of what were actually chamber pots at night. But hunger drives, and we were so starved that we were ready to eat any food. . . ."

An average man needs about 4,800 calories per day to perform heavy labor, about 3,600 calories for ordinary work. The average Auschwitz prisoner, by official postwar estimates that remain very uncertain, received about 1,500. Many often got no more than half that amount. Apart from calories, of course, there were gross shortages of vitamins and minerals. Scurvy and skin diseases soon became commonplace. Starving children suffered strange afflictions like noma, a gangrenous ulceration that creates gaping holes through the cheek. "I saw diseases which you find only in textbooks," Dr. Lingens testified at the Frankfurt trial. "I never thought I'd see any of them—for example, phemphicus, a very rare disease, in which large areas of the skin become detached and the patient dies within a few days."

The basic effect of starvation, though, is simply emaciation and exhaustion. The body feeds on itself, first on the fat and then on the muscles, which become soft and waste away. "The face looked like a mask," Nutrition Professor J. Olbrycht

testified on the condition of these prisoners at Hoess' trial in
Cracow, "with a faraway look in the eyes and the pupils
unnaturally enlarged. There was apathy and sleepiness, the
slowing down and weakening of all life processes." The
Auschwitz prisoners easily recognized these marks of coming death, and with the stinging acerbity of the death camps,
they likened the numbed victims to the starving beggars of
India and named them *Musselmänner*, or Moslems. "Such sick
people saw and heard badly," Dr. Olbrycht's testimony continued, "perception, thinking, and all reactions were slowed
down, . . . hence, also, lethargy in carrying out instructions,
wrongly interpreted as evidence of passive resistance." What
Dr. Olbrycht meant was that the starving "Moslems" couldn't
carry out or even understand the orders barked at them by
their guardians, and so they were frequently punished for
insubordination and beaten to death.

As a self-contained universe, Auschwitz required and
provided work of every sort. The camp had its own bakery
and its own tannery and its own tinsmithy. Most of the work,
however, was simply brute labor, devoted to the constant
expansions of the camp for the constant acquisition of new
prisoners. One huge earth-rolling machine required sixty
prisoners to haul it along for the building of new roadbeds,
and when all the horses at the Babice farm were requisitioned
by the military in the spring of 1944, teams of women prisoners
were harnessed like animals to the plows. The building went
on unremittingly until the very end; a new set of barracks
known as "Mexico" was still under construction when the SS
dynamited the camp and departed. "We work beneath the
earth and above it," Borowski wrote, "under a roof and in the
rain, with the spade, the pickax and the crowbar. We carry
huge sacks of cement, lay bricks, put down rails, spread
gravel, trample the earth . . . We are laying the foundation for

some new, monstrous civilization. Only now do I realize what price was paid for building ancient civilizations. . . . How much blood must have poured onto the Roman roads, the bulwarks, and the city walls. Antiquity—the tremendous concentration camp where the slave was branded on the forehead by his master, and crucified for trying to escape . . . ! Roman law! Yes, today too there is a law!"

Under the New Order, as in the slave states of the past, such labor could be sold. Many prominent German corporations—among them Krupp, Siemens and Bayer—were interested in what might be negotiated. Auschwitz began developing a network of outlying subcamps, thirty-four in all. The prisoners worked at a cement plant in Goleszow, a coal mine in Wesola, a steel factory in Gliwice, a shoe factory in Chelmek. In the subcamp called Tschechowitz I, the prisoners' main occupation was to remove the fuses from bombs that had failed to explode during Allied air raids. Working conditions in all these places were unbearable. "For interminable days on end, I pushed coal-laden carts up those long, dimly lit corridors, beaten like a donkey en route," a French boxer named Sim Kessel recalled of the coal mines at Jaworzno. The prisoners' only breakfast was a bowl of hot water, divided among four men, before the descent into the sweltering mines. "In the intense heat of those galleries, our raging thirst often drove us to drink our own urine," Kessel said. "We all did. We would urinate into our cupped hands and then drink it. . . ."

The biggest of these Auschwitz subcamps was the I. G. Farben plant first started at Dwory and then headquartered in Monowitz. The plant was known as Buna because its principal purpose was to produce synthetic rubber; its other main installation was a hydrogenation plant designed to convert coal into oil at a rate of nearly 800,000 tons a month. The

Farben directors were so impressed with the possibilities of
their Auschwitz factories—particularly when they contemplated the victorious end of the war and the whole East
European market lying open before them—that they insisted
on turning aside all government grants and financing the
Auschwitz plants themselves. They committed 900 million
marks (about $225 million) to the project, which made the
Auschwitz factories the largest in the Farben empire. The SS
agreed to provide all necessary labor, for a modest fee. It
charged Farben four marks ($1) per day for each skilled
worker, three marks for each unskilled one. Later in the war,
the SS agreed to provide child laborers for one and a half
marks.

Conditions at Monowitz were much like those at
Auschwitz—the dawn roll calls, the starvation rations, the
labor gangs sent out for twelve hours at a time, forced to
work at the double, beaten by guards, harried by giant dogs.
The prisoners who died of overwork—dozens of them every
day—had to be hauled back to camp at nightfall so that they
could be propped up and counted at the next morning's roll
call. About 25,000 people, ultimately, were killed in the construction of the I. G. Farben plant at Monowitz. One of the
enduring mysteries of Auschwitz is that this plant, built at
such cost and such suffering, never actually produced one
ounce of synthetic rubber.*

Of the three or four marks paid daily to the SS for a prisoner's labor, the prisoner, of course, never received a pfennig.

---

* One section of the Monowitz plant did start producing four truckloads per
day of synthetic gasoline early in 1944, but the facility was knocked out by a
U.S. air raid that summer. The damage was repaired in a month. A second
air raid soon after that halted production permanently.

The stripped and plundered Auschwitz prisoners were not allowed to own anything. And so, inevitably, the desire to possess things became a passion exceeded only by the desire to eat and the desire to be safe. "I badly needed a waistband to hold up my drawers," Olga Lengyel later recalled. "At the garbage dump, by a wonderful stroke of luck, I found three fragments of twine which could be pieced together for the purpose. I also found a flat piece of wood, which I could sharpen into a knife. . . . These new acquisitions filled me with pride. I felt that I had become a rich woman in the camp."

From the instinct to possess comes the instinct to trade, and so there arose the vast black market around "Canada," with its canned hams, its carpets, its stamp collections, perfumes and antique clocks. Since the SS men were corrupt, and the *Kapos* were corrupt, and the prisoners who had survived would do almost anything to go on surviving, everything was for sale. Even the gold bars melted down from the teeth of the victims of the crematoria, supposedly destined for the national bank in Berlin, often ended on the black market. But the chief black-market areas were the latrines and the garbage dump, where prisoners bargained over pieces of stale bread.

"The Market is always very active," wrote Primo Levi. "Although every exchange (in fact, every form of possession) is explicitly forbidden . . . the northeast corner of the *Lager* . . . is permanently occupied by a tumultuous throng, in the open during the summer, in a washroom during the winter, as soon as the squads return from work. Here scores of prisoners driven desperate by hunger prowl around, with lips half open and eyes gleaming . . . " Olga Lengyel has even preserved some of the prices quoted in the latrines of Auschwitz: A kilo of margarine was worth 250 gold marks, or about $60. One kilo of butter: 500 marks. One kilo of meat: 1,000 marks. A cigarette cost seven marks, but the price of a single puff could be negotiated. So could the price of sex. Officially, none was permitted; unofficially, life continued. Primo Levi watched closely the fluctuations of supply and demand. "While there is a virtually stable price for soup (half a ration of bread for two pints)," he wrote, "the quotations for turnips, carrots, potatoes are extremely variable and depend greatly, among other factors, on the diligence and corruptibility of the guards at the stores."

Since the official rations, reduced by SS thievery, condemned every prisoner to eventual death by starvation, survival depended on a prisoner's ability to "organize" extra supplies for himself and to find himself a sanctuary in the hospital or the kitchens or in some other relatively protected quarter. Assignment to the coal mines at Jaworzno meant almost certain death; assignment to some administrative office meant at least the possibility of survival. "No prisoner who came to Auschwitz before the summer of 1944 survived unless he held a special job," Dr. Lingens testified.

Out of this struggle for survival, therefore, emerged a prison hierarchy, a hierarchy in which men who lived on the brink of death managed to edge away from that brink by edging past other prisoners.

The hierarchy expressed itself in symbols, all designed to contradict the symbolism of the SS. Just as the SS degraded the prisoners by ordering them to wear shapeless rags, the most resilient and imaginative prisoners fought back by commissioning captive tailors to dress them in the most beautifully fitted prison costumes. Among the women, similarly, prestige attended anyone whose shaved skull began to grow hair again, or who appeared at work in a handsome skirt. All these self-assertions were forbidden, of course, and therefore anyone who appeared in full-grown hair or attractive clothing was assumed to be under someone's protection, a member of the hierarchy. Fania Fénelon, a French girl who played in the women's orchestra at Birkenau, has described an extraordinary night on which the prostitutes who dominated the prisoner hierarchy in the women's camp gave a big party for themselves. They hired the whole orchestra to play dance music in exchange for leftover sausages and sauerkraut. Some of the women, Mademoiselle Fénelon recalled, had arrayed themselves in their Berlin street finery, black lace underwear and transparent blouses, while others had dressed up as men, sporting silk pajamas. Then they danced and drank and pawed at each other. "Everywhere women were hugging, kissing and caressing," she wrote, "lying flat out on tables, sliding to the floor . . . " The night of these festivities was the night on which the SS suddenly liquidated the gypsy compound.

The hierarchy extended from such privileged prisoners upward through the bellicose block seniors and barracks overseers and on to the mighty *Kapos*, who had once been, most of them, common criminals. "These *Kapos* . . . were the aristocrats of the camps," recalled one Auschwitz prisoner, Rudolf Vrba. "They had their own rooms in each barracks, and there they entertained their friends to splendid meals. They cooked steaks and chips on their stoves, while the smell wafted through thin partitions to starving prisoners, and they washed it down occasionally with slivovitz stolen from victims of the gas chambers."

The *Kapos* were never safe, however, from the ferocity of the SS. If any of them faltered, he could be instantly reduced to the ranks of common prisoners, and he knew very well what revenge awaited him in the barracks at night. ("We . . . dragged him onto the cement floor under the stove," Borowski wrote of one such retribution, "where the entire block, grunting and growling, trampled him to death.") In the eyes of the Nazis, the *Kapos* who strutted about with their clubs remained no more than criminals, useful in performing the disciplinary chores in whatever way best suited the camp's reigning aristocracy, the SS.

The SS was the self-proclaimed elite not only of Auschwitz but of Nazi Germany and thus all Europe. Founded in 1925 as a kind of bodyguard for Hitler, the SS had only 280 members when Himmler took it over in 1929. He emphasized its supposedly privileged status, its preference for blond and blue-eyed recruits, its exotic black uniforms. "I swear to you, Adolf Hitler, loyalty and valor," each of the SS men vowed. "I pledge to you ... obedience unto death, so help me God." Himmler took charge of the concentration camps almost from the beginning, and by the time the war began he had created a private army of 250,000 men, including more than a few of the petty criminals he professed to despise. The SS forces at Auschwitz were never large— about 3,000 men to oversee a prison camp of nearly 150,000— but their immaculate uniforms, their guns and whips, and their guard dogs, gave them an aura of invincibility.

To the SS men themselves, duty at Auschwitz was chiefly an unpleasant assignment that kept them from the far more unpleasant prospect of combat on the Russian front. In the east, one could get killed; at Auschwitz, one got extra rations for taking part in one of the gassings known as "special actions"—one fifth of a liter of vodka, five cigarettes, one hundred grams of sausage. At more elevated levels of the SS hierarchy, the rewards were even more generous. Dr. Johann Paul Kremer, a professor of anatomy in Münster, kept a diary of his service in Poland in the fall of 1942, devoting only a few sentences to his role in the "special actions" but savoring the good life at Auschwitz, particularly the good food served at the Waffen SS club. Thus: "September 6, 1942: Today an excellent Sunday dinner: tomato soup, one half of chicken with potatoes and red cabbage, and magnificent vanilla ice cream. . . . September 17: Have ordered a casual coat from Berlin. . . . September 20: This Sunday afternoon I listened from 3 P.M. till 6 P.M. to a concert of the prisoners' band in glorious sunshine; the bandmaster was a conductor of the State Opera from Warsaw. Eighty musicians. Roast pork for dinner. . . . September 23: . . . a truly festive meal. We had baked pike, as much of it as we wanted, real coffee, excellent beer and sandwiches. . . . September 27: This Sunday afternoon, from 4 till 8, a party in the club with supper, free beer and cigarettes. Speech of Commandant Hoess and a musical and theatrical program. . . . October 11: For dinner roast hare, a whole fat haunch, with dumplings and red cabbage. . . . October 31: Very beautiful autumn weather for the last fourteen days, so that every day one has the opportunity of sunbathing in the garden of the Waffen SS clubhouse. . . . November 8: . . . we had Bulgarian red wine and plum brandy from Croatia. . . . November 14: Today, Saturday, a variety theater performance in the mess room (quite grand!). The dancing dogs excited great enthusiasm and so did the bantam cocks which crowed in unison. . . ."

The isolation of the SS men, who lived above and beyond all the rules of survival that governed the starving prisoners, enabled them to act on whim, to decide questions of life and death on impulse. Thus the strange salvation of Sim Kessel, the French boxer, who had been selected for the gas chambers. "Now we were ordered to take off our clothes and lay them neatly folded along the wall," Kessel later recalled. "We did so. There we skeletons stood barefoot in the snow . . . " A detachment of SS men roared up on motorcycles, simply to oversee the shipment of these walking corpses to the gas chambers. The naked prisoners stood in the snow and waited. Then Kessel noticed that one of the SS men, a non-com, had a broken nose, and ridges of scar tissue over the eyes, and all the other marks of the ring. "I hesitated for a second and then thought, Oh, what the hell! Naked and shivering, I walked up to him [and] simply blurted out in German, 'Boxer?'

"'Boxer? Ja!'

"He didn't wait for me to explain, he understood. I too had a broken nose." The SS man asked Kessel where he had fought, and Kessel named a series of second-rate places, Pacra, Central, Delbor, Japy. The SS man gave a quick smile of recognition, then ordered Kessel to climb aboard his motorcycle so that he could drive him to the sanctuary of the hospital. "It must have been a weird and unforgettable sight," Kessel observed, "the pathetic nude prisoner riding behind an SS on the back seat of a motorcycle, running right through the center of Auschwitz. . . . I never saw him again."

This same whimsical turn of fate, once the SS had decided to break all its own rules, touched an Austrian leftist named Rudolf Friemel, who had fought in the defense of Madrid, then escaped to France, then been arrested and eventually shipped to Auschwitz. While in France, he had become involved with a French woman named Margarita Ferrer Rey, who had borne him a son, and who now demanded that he marry her. Her demand somehow penetrated the machinery of the Nazi state and floated upward to the highest levels, perhaps to Himmler, perhaps to Hitler himself. From the highest levels, the order came down, decreeing that Mademoiselle Rey and her son should be taken to the "labor camp" at Auschwitz so that she could be married and her son legitimized. Such sponsorship inspired the Auschwitz authorities to the most elaborate preparations. Friemel was stripped of his prison rags and outfitted with a new suit that had been specially ironed by the *Kapo* in the laundry room. He was even issued a necktie and matching socks. Somewhere a priest was found to marry the Austrian and his bride. Then they had their matrimonial picture taken by a technician from the Auschwitz photo lab, she with a bouquet of hyacinths in her arms. A group of musicians from the Auschwitz orchestra played appropriate tunes. The newlyweds then went to the camp brothel, which had been emptied of its regular inhabitants in honor of the wedding night. The next day, the Frenchwoman and her son were shipped back to France, and the Austrian was put back into his prison uniform and returned to his work gang.

At the top of the hierarchy, of course, was the camp commandant, who lived with his wife, Hedwig, and their five children in a tree-shaded stucco house known as Villa Hoess. It stood just outside the northeastern corner of the camp, separated from the neighboring barracks by a concrete wall high enough so that nothing inside the camp could actually be seen by Hoess' family. Near the wall, Frau Hoess grew rose hedges, and begonias in blue flowerboxes. "My wife's garden was a paradise of flowers . . ." the commandant recalled. "No former prisoner can ever say that he was in any way or at any time badly treated in our house. My wife's greatest pleasure would have been to give a present to every prisoner who was in any way connected with our household. The children were perpetually begging me for cigarettes for the prisoners. . . . The children always kept animals in the garden, creatures the prisoners were forever bringing them. Tortoises, martens, cats, lizards. . . . Their greatest joy was when Daddy bathed with them [in the swimming pool]. He had, however, so little time for all these childish pleasures. . . . "

The image of the Villa Hoess as a plantation tended by

devoted prisoners is about as accurate as Hoess' image of himself as a sternly incorruptible soldier. Stanislaw Dubiel, who somehow managed to remain a gardener to the rulers of Auschwitz from 1940 to 1945, testified that the Hoesses limited themselves neither to their rations nor to their incomes but rather extorted everything they wanted from the SS hierarchy. "I took from the [prisoners' food] magazine for the Hoess household: sugar, flour, margarine, various baking powders, condiments for soup, macaroni, oat flakes, cocoa, cinnamon, cream of wheat, peas and other foodstuffs. Frau Hoess never had enough of them.... I also supplied the Hoess kitchen with meat from the butcher's, and always with milk.... Frau Hoess would very often also demand cream.... Hoess never paid for the provisions taken from the prisoners' food store, or from the camp butcher's.... The equipment and furnishings of the Hoess home were of similar origin. Everything was made by prisoners from camp materials. The rooms were furnished with the most magnificent furniture, the desk drawers were covered with leather.... Two Jewish dressmakers were employed in the Hoess home [to make] dresses for Frau Hoess and her daughters.... Hoess settled down in such a well-appointed and magnificent home that his wife remarked, *'Hier will ich leben und sterben* (I want to live here till I die).'"

Hoess' self-portrait as a devoted paterfamilias is also somewhat exaggerated. He had an affair with an Italian prisoner named Eleonore Hodys, who worked for several months in the Villa Hoess. He tried then to get rid of her by assigning her to the penal company, in which death within a few weeks by overwork and mistreatment was taken for granted. Then she was mysteriously transferred to the stifling dungeons of Block 11. There Hoess secretly visited her. There she became pregnant. When Hoess heard of her pregnancy, he ordered her gassed. "Into the chimney with her," he commanded, according to a witness at the Frankfurt trial. But the chief of Block 11, Max Grabner, who was already being investigated for having an affair with a prisoner, became interested in Eleonore Hodys and informed on Hoess to that same SS Judge Morgen who was pursuing the Grabner case. Morgen apparently rescued Eleonore Hodys from Auschwitz and sent her to Munich, though the SS killed her toward the end of the war.

But Hoess' children, to whom the servile prisoners brought presents, understood their father and the world he ruled. A French prisoner named Charlotte Delbo caught a glimpse of that understanding and recorded a matchless image of the commandant's sons at play. She saw two boys, aged about eleven and seven, both blond and blue-eyed. The older one had a sword in his belt, and he screwed an imaginary monocle into his eye as he ordered the younger one, who represented all the prisoners in the camp, to march faster and faster. "Soon the prisoners to whom these orders are addressed can no longer follow. They stumble on the ground, lose their footing. Their commandant is pale with rage. With his switch, he strikes, strikes, strikes. He screams in rage, '*Schnell! Schneller!*' . . . The little boy staggers, spins around, and falls flat on the grass. The commandant looks at the prisoner that he has knocked to the ground with contempt, saliva on his lips. And his fury subsides. He feels only disgust. He kicks him—a fake kick, he is barefoot and he's just playing. But the little boy knows the game. The kick turns him over like a limp bag. He lies there, mouth open, eyes glazed over. Then the big boy, with a sign of the stick to the invisible prisoners that surround him, commands, '*Zum Krematorium,*' and moves on. Stiff, satisfied, and disgusted."

*

In theory, there were no children in Auschwitz. All of them were supposed to be singled out on the railroad ramp, judged unfit for hard labor, and sent directly to the gas chambers. Some survived that process, for various reasons, but eventually the process caught them.

Dunja Wasserstrom, a Russian woman who ended as a language teacher in Mexico, testified at the Frankfurt trial about one such case. As a prisoner, she had the misfortune to work for Friedrich Wilhelm Boger, Grabner's deputy in the Auschwitz Gestapo, who made her watch while he interrogated suspects on a whirling contraption known as "the Boger swing." One day, there was an interlude.

"A truck came and stopped for a moment in front of the Political Section," Mrs. Wasserstrom testified. "A little boy jumped off. He held an apple in his hand. Boger and Draser [another SS man] were standing in the doorway. I was standing at the window. The child was standing next to the car with his apple and was enjoying himself. Suddenly Boger went over to the boy, grabbed his legs, and smashed his head against the wall. Then he calmly picked up the apple. And Draser told me to wipe 'that' off the wall. About an hour later I was called to Boger to interpret in an interrogation, and I saw him eating the child's apple."

The Frankfurt court had heard a good deal of testimony about the enormities of Auschwitz, but it found this small scene hard to believe.

"You saw this with your own eyes?" the witness was asked.

"I saw it with my own eyes," she said.

"You can swear to it in good conscience?"

"Absolutely."

The children who survived the ramp at Auschwitz soon learned and understood what was going to happen to them.

The first Auschwitz prisoner to testify at Frankfurt, Dr. Otto Wolken, sixty, a general practitioner in Vienna, told of having encountered a boy in the dispensary and of having asked him, "Well, boy, how are you? Are you afraid?" The boy answered, "I am not afraid. Everything here is so terrible it can only be better up there."

Then Wolken told of having heard an SS man talking to a boy of about ten through a barbed-wire barrier. The SS man said, "Well, my boy, you know a lot for your age." The boy answered, "I know that I know a lot, and I also know that I won't learn any more."

Then Wolken told of a group of ninety children who arrived in Auschwitz and were placed in quarantine for several days and then were loaded onto trucks to go to the gas chambers.

"There was one boy, a little older than the rest," Wolken testified, "who called out to them when they resisted, 'Climb into the car, don't scream. You saw how your parents and grandparents were gassed. We'll see them again up there.' And then he turned to the SS men and shouted, 'But don't think you'll get away with it. You'll die the way you let us die.' He was a brave boy. In this moment he said what he had to say."

*

At Christmastime, a large Christmas tree was erected opposite one of the crematoria. It was decorated with colored lights. The prisoners were ordered to sing "Silent Night." Anyone who did not sing it correctly got no evening rations.

*

The gas chamber was, in a sense, the easiest fate. Life ended quickly there, whereas the various punishments devised by the SS achieved the same end more slowly and

more painfully. Aside from the routine starvation and mistreatment, the most standard of these punishments was public flogging, usually a minimum of twenty-five blows on the
bared buttocks with a whip or wooden club. The victim was
often forced to count each blow aloud, and if he failed to
keep count the flogging started again from the beginning.
When the ordeal ended, the prisoner was often unconscious,
and the bruises on his thighs were frequently so severe that
he never recovered.

Even flogging might be considered preferable to the torments inflicted in Block 11. The Gestapo had endless questions to ask, about the camp underground, about escape
attempts, about links to the resistance movement, and it
accepted no pleas of ignorance. "The atmosphere was oppres-
sive," recalled Sim Kessel, who had originally been arrested
while smuggling guns for the French resistance. "Almost
bare walls with only a picture of Der Führer and the
swastika, plus a few shelves holding books and files. For furniture, two massive tables, some straight-backed chairs.
Seated at the tables were four men smoking. The youngest,
short and blond, was drinking a cup of steaming coffee. . . ."

There came then the standard questioning, and then the
standard beating, until the blood poured from Kessel's ears
and nose. Then the guards flung him into a chair facing the
short, blond SS man, who held a medical kit in his lap. "With
finicky deliberation he took out pliers and scalpels of various
sizes," Kessel recalled, "looking at me at the same time, he
smiled gently as if he were setting up a game. . . . Finally he
took a small pair of pliers, picked up my left hand and
applied the instrument to the nail of my middle finger, driving one tong of the tool under the nail to get a better grip.
Then he pulled. I screamed. He paused for an instant, smiling
all the while, then pulled again. I watched the nail come out

slowly, millimeter by millimeter. He never stopped smiling. . . . 'Well, Kessel, had enough?'"

Gestapo Deputy Boger's favorite method involved the so-called Boger swing, a device of his own invention. "My talking machine will make you talk," he used to tell the prisoners. The swing consisted of a steel bar to which the prisoner was tied by his wrists and ankles. As Boger lunged at him with his club, usually aiming for the genitals, the prisoner swung head over heels, round and round. One prisoner named Breiden, who came to testify at the Frankfurt trial, burst into tears on the witness stand when he saw a replica of the machine to which he had once been bound. "Murderer!" he shouted at Boger.

"Terrible cries could be heard," said another witness, Maryla Rosenthal, who had to work in an adjoining room. "After an hour or more the victims would be carried out on a stretcher. They no longer looked human. I could not recognize them." One reasonably typical victim was a prisoner from Munich named Gustl Berger. He and another prisoner named Rohmann were accused of having acquired some alcohol from the SS canteen. Rohmann was confined to one of the *Stehzelle*, or standing cells. These were vertical tubes, about three feet by three feet across, in which the prisoner could neither sit nor lie. Nor was he fed. "The door never opened," said a Polish prisoner named Josef Kral, who actually survived the standing cells. "One could shout and curse Hitler and everybody else. Nobody would come. Death from hunger is not an easy death. . . . The prisoners screamed, begged, pleaded, licked the walls . . . "

Rohmann lasted nineteen days, according to the testimony of a Munich businessman named Paul Leo Scheidel, and then he "starved to death, finis, gone." But from Berger the Gestapo wanted to know how the alcohol had been obtained, and so he was tied to the Boger swing. After forty-five minutes, according to Scheidel's testimony, "the skin on his hands was gone, his buttocks were ripped open, his face was smeared with blood." After his interrogation, Berger was led out into the yard outside Block 11, where the Nazis had built a wall of black cork as the backdrop for thousands of summary executions. In front of the wall lay a bed of sand to soak up the blood that gushed from the victims. "You murderers! You criminals!" Berger shouted. Then Boger shot him.

It might seem that nothing could be worse than Block 11, but Block 10 may have been even worse. This was where the SS doctors assembled the prisoners who had been selected for various medical experiments. There seems to have been very little purpose or coherence to these experiments. Anyone in Germany who had some quasi-scientific proposal that might benefit the state could send his suggestion to Himmler's headquarters in Berlin, and in due time authorizations of one sort or another would be issued. Some of these proposals were relatively innocuous, and so we find the pharmaceutical firm of Bayer asking for "a number of women in connection with our intended experiments with a new sleeping drug." Other schemes were both lethal and utterly pointless, like the request from Professor Hirt of the University of Strasbourg that the heads of 150 "Jewish-Bolshevist commisars, who embody a repulsive but characteristic subhumanity," be cut off and sent to Strasbourg for study. Or like Dr. Mengele's obsessive efforts to explore the mysteries of twins. Dr. Miklos Nyiszli, a Hungarian prisoner who served as Mengele's pathologist, reported that "several hundred sets of twins" turned up in Auschwitz. Mengele, who seems to have thought that he was seeking methods to increase the German birth rate, ordered each pair carefully examined and then killed. Since twins do not ordinarily die simultaneously, Mengele considered himself blessed with a rare research opportunity, and he rushed the results of all the autopsies to the Institute of Biological, Racial and Evolutionary Research in Berlin.

The main medical experiments in Auschwitz dealt with sterilization. Officially, the goal was to refine the program of genocide by not simply killing the members of "inferior races" but first sterilizing them and then putting them to work. As early as March 28, 1941, before the Final Solution was decreed, an SS official named Viktor Brack was urging Himmler to have all able-bodied Jews sterilized by X rays. Brack's theory was that the unwitting victims should be made to line up at a counter. "There," he wrote, "they would be asked questions or handed a form to fill in, keeping them at the counter for two or three minutes. The clerk behind the counter would . . . start an X-ray apparatus with two tubes to irradiate the persons at the counter . . . " At Auschwitz, as Hoess said, everything was possible. Dr. Horst Schumann of Berlin exposed a batch of several hundred Dutch and Greek Jews to fifteen minutes of radiation of the genital area at a rate of thirty prisoners a day. Many victims suffered severe burns. After three months, Dr. Schumann removed parts of the women's sexual organs to be sent to Berlin for analysis. The men were castrated. Records of these experiments were partially destroyed, but one surviving report from one day in the surgical ward, December 16, 1943, records ninety castrations.

Himmler had meanwhile met Professor Carl Clauberg of the University of Königsberg, who ran a clinic for the treatment of sterile women. Himmler asked Dr. Clauberg whether he could turn his knowledge to the opposite side of the problem and devise a technique of mass sterilization. Clauberg was delighted with the prospect of official support for his research and unlimited numbers of patients to work on. When he arrived at Auschwitz in the spring of 1943, more than two hundred women were installed in Block 10 and placed at his disposal. Clauberg injected various chemicals into their Fallopian tubes. His formulas were kept secret, but the main ingredient was apparently a formalin solution. This stopped the women's menstruation. Clauberg pronounced his system a great success. He boasted to Himmler that his method would enable one skilled physician with ten assistants to sterilize several hundred women a day.

After the completion of these experiments, the subjects were generally sent to the gas chambers.

*

The worst crime that a prisoner could commit at Auschwitz, and therefore the crime most sternly punished, was to attempt an escape. This was very difficult but not impossible, for cunning, strength and bribery all had an effect. There were more than six hundred cases. Once the roll call disclosed that someone was missing, the sirens began wailing, and everything stopped. The prisoners had to stand at attention for hours while detachments of SS men set forth with their dogs to hunt for the fugitive. For as long as three days, the hunt continued through all the fields and marshes that surrounded Auschwitz. About two thirds of the time, the pursuers soon found their prey. After torturing him to make him confess who had helped him escape, the SS made him parade around the camp with a sign that said, "Hurrah! I'm back!" Then they gathered all the other prisoners to watch his punishment, and they hanged him.

There was a remarkable young woman in Birkenau named Mala Zimetbaum, aged about twenty, tattooed with the number 19880. She was Polish by birth, but her family migrated to Belgium, to Antwerp, and there, after her father went blind, she dropped out of school to help support him and the four other children. When the Germans overran Belgium, she joined the resistance but was soon arrested and shipped to Auschwitz. There she became a *Läuferin*, or runner, someone who carried messages and ran errands all over the camp. That enabled her to do favors and to tip off the prisoners whenever a selection was planned. One Auschwitz survivor remembered her as "the one who tried to make it easier for us when we arrived." Everybody loved her for her courage and independence, for a spirit that even the SS men respected.

Now Mala fell in love with a young Pole named Edek Galiński, also a member of the resistance, and Edek figured out a scheme to escape from Auschwitz. He found a way to steal an SS uniform, but he needed an SS pass, which only Mala, making her rounds of the camp, could find and acquire. Mala was perfectly willing to get him the pass but pleaded with him to take her along. He agreed.

On June 24, 1944, Edek Galiński marched out of Auschwitz in the uniform of an SS man. At the gate, he displayed documents declaring that he was authorized to take with him the female prisoner who was in his custody. Having performed this impossible feat, Mala and Edek seem to have lost all sense of who and where they were. Although accounts of their wanderings differ, they seem to have walked to the nearby town of Kozy, and there they found themselves a room and made love. Then they trekked on to Cracow. They apparently thought that their SS papers made them invisible, or immune to the laws of Auschwitz. For several weeks, they survived in this absurd defiance, and then an SS man accosted them in a café and asked to see their papers and refused to accept the faked papers that they offered him.

Another version, told at the Eichmann trial by a survivor

named Raja Kagan, reported that they were caught trying to
cross the frontier into Slovakia. They had asked some cus-
toms officers for directions, she said, and the officers became
suspicious "that anyone in an SS uniform would come to ask
for the road." According to yet another account, the two fugi-
tives never got beyond Kozy.

Their escape, in any case, electrified the camp. "Every
community has its legend, its myth," said a prisoner named
Lena Berg. "That of Auschwitz was a romance involving Mala,
a girl who worked as a messenger, and her lover, a Warsaw
Pole. . . . To all of us this [escape] was an impossible dream
come true, and the prisoners' pinched, starved faces lit up with
smiles. Mala's fate became our main concern. They had
escaped, we told ourselves; they were free and happy. A few
weeks later we learned that they had been caught, and were
being kept in an underground dungeon and tortured to reveal
the names of those who had helped them to escape. The man
insisted that he alone was responsible. . . ." Fania Fénelon, who
played in the camp orchestra, was even more emotional. She
recalled that it was Mala who had spread the news of the
Allied landing in Normandy just a few days earlier, and now,
she said, the prisoners indulged in fantasies of the two fugi-
tives leading the forces that would liberate them. "We were
insanely gleeful," she wrote later. "Our reasoning was over-
simple but heartening: 'Since they're out, we'll be freed!' We
were beside ourselves. . . . We could already see Mala and
Edek returning at the head of millions of soldiers, who would
enter the camp and put out the SS men's eyes, bayonet them in
the stomach. We were drunk with images of gory revenge. For
the first time since our internment we lived and breathed
hope. . . . There were vicious searches throughout the camps,
interrogations in the SS building, accomplices were sought. But
everyone claimed ignorance, and it was true."

The prisoners were assembled on August 22 to watch Mala, battered and bloodied by the Gestapo, go to the gallows. She refused to carry the sign rejoicing in her recapture. They could not make her do that. But the commander of the Birkenau women's camp, Marie Mandel, looked triumphant as she began reading out the death sentence. "Mala stood . . . pale and calm," Lena Berg recalled, "and the hearts of the thousands of women who watched her pounded with hers. She had disappointed them when her audacious dream of happiness had collapsed, but she was not going to disappoint them now." While Marie Mandel read the death sentence, Mala suddenly produced from somewhere a razor blade and slashed her wrist. An SS man named Riters grabbed her arm and tried to stop her. Mala managed to strike one last blow in her own defense: She smashed the SS man in the face with her bloody fist.

"Get away from me, you dirty dog," she cried.

"You stupid Jewish whore!" the SS man snarled as he struggled with her. "So you thought you'd kill yourself, but that's what we're here for!"

"Murderers!" Mala cried out. "You will soon pay for our suffering! Don't be afraid, girls! Their end is near. I am certain of that. I know. I was free!"

A half-dozen SS men threw themselves on Mala, clubbed her to the ground, kicked her prostrate body and flung her into the back of a waiting truck that took her to the crematorium.

On the other side of the camp, a similar ceremony awaited Edek Galiński. He was bloodied almost beyond recognition by the Gestapo men in Block 11, but in the middle of the reading of the death sentence he leaped onto a bench, thrust his head into the waiting noose, and then kicked over the bench. The SS men rescued him too, then hanged him

themselves. His last words were an unfinished cry of defiance: "Long live the Po—"

*

It may seem absurd to report that life in hell could gradu-
ally improve, but there is much testimony to confirm that
conditions in Auschwitz did get somewhat better during
1943 and early 1944. "At the beginning, beating and killing
were the rule, but later this became only sporadic," Borowski
wrote as he listed the new comforts. "At first you had to
sleep on the floor lying on your side because of the lack of
space, and could turn over only on command; later you slept
in bunks, or wherever you wished, sometimes even in bed.
Originally, you had to stand at roll call for as long as two
days at a time, later only until the second gong, until nine
o'clock. In the early years, packages were forbidden, later
you could receive five hundred grams, and finally as much as
you wanted . . . Life in the camp became 'better and better'
all the time—after the first three or four years. We felt certain
that the horrors could never again be repeated, and we were
proud that we had survived."

One reason for the change may be that Rudolf Hoess won
a promotion in November of 1943 and was summoned back
to Berlin to become inspector of concentration camps. Into his
place as commandant at Auschwitz stepped SS Lieutenant
Colonel Arthur Liebehenschel. He was a rather small, pudgy
man with bulging eyes and a weak, dissolute face, and yet he
asserted from the beginning a series of modest changes and
reforms. He made an inspection tour of Block 11 and ordered
fifty-six of the captives released from their dark cells and
returned to the regular camp. He abolished the standing cells.
He canceled the rule decreeing the death penalty for any
attempt at escape, and the rule imposing collective responsibility on all prisoners for any such attempt. He reduced the

power of the professional criminals who wore the green triangles, and gave more authority to the leftists and other political prisoners who wore the red triangles. Whether these mild
reforms were the result of his own wishes or of orders from
Berlin remains uncertain, but his arrival was only part of an
organizational upheaval at Auschwitz. While Hoess himself
went on to a bigger job in Berlin, his chief deputies were
brought down by the strange subterranean currents of SS politics. Not only was Gestapo Chief Max Grabner embroiled in
an SS investigation, but so was Rapportführer Gerhard
Pallitzsch, one of the five SS officers from Sachsenhausen who
had accompanied Hoess on his original trip to Auschwitz.
Pallitzsch was suddenly shipped off to be commandant of a
small subcamp in Brno, Czechoslovakia, then arrested three
weeks later on a charge of having had an affair with a Jewish
prisoner at Birkenau, then sent to join an SS combat unit
fighting Hungarian partisans. He was killed near Budapest.

Though these upheavals may all have been a matter of SS
politics, those politics themselves were changing as a conse-
quence of one increasingly important fact: The German victory, on which everything was predicated, no longer seemed
so certain. General Paulus' Sixth Army had been surrounded
and besieged in Stalingrad, and after nearly three months of
house-to-house combat in the ruins of the snow-covered city,
Paulus surrendered on January 31, 1943. The retreat from
Russia was irreversible. At the other end of Hitler's empire,
the Americans and the British had invaded Morocco in
November of 1942 and conquered all of North Africa by the
following May, then invaded Sicily in July. Such events forced
even the most dedicated of SS officers to wonder about their
own futures, to wonder how their own actions might someday be judged, and who might survive to bear witness
against them. The *Kapos*, who actually ran the concentration

camps much of the time and inflicted much of the hardship on the ordinary prisoners, must have felt similar misgivings.

There has been speculation, particularly among East Europeans, that the slaughter of the Jews was only the first stage of an extermination campaign that would eventually extend to the Poles and the Slavs and all other "inferior" peoples who interfered with Hitler's dream of German colonization of the east. If that was indeed Hitler's plan, the changing fortunes of war necessarily stayed his hand, but they did not by any means bring a modification of the Final Solution. On the contrary, the difficulties caused by the war, the shortages of transportation and fuel—all these inspired the SS officers in command of the annihilation not to reduce their efforts but to intensify them, to get their assignment finished before they could be prevented from carrying it out at all. What this meant at Auschwitz was that life got better for the camp inmates because the inmates were mostly Gentiles (about three quarters of them), and after about June of 1943 the Nazis stopped gassing Gentiles. They could still be shot, of course, for any number of offenses, from attempting escape to stealing a piece of bread. But the SS now concentrated its efforts on the destruction of the Jews.

For this, Auschwitz was reorganized again. In May of 1944, Rudolf Hoess reassumed command of the camp he had created, but he exercised only a general supervision. Direct command over Auschwitz was delegated to Richard Baer, and over Birkenau to Josef Kramer, two killers worthy of the task ahead. The milder Liebehenschel was transferred to Majdanek, which was already in the process of closing down.

The next step was to renovate the giant crematoria, to repair all cracks in the brickwork, to reinforce the chimneys with steel bands, to repaint the "changing rooms," to prepare all the machinery for maximum use. The railroad line was extended into Birkenau so that prisoners could be unloaded within two hundred yards of the crematoria, rather than being trucked over from the main camp at Auschwitz. The culmination of the Holocaust, the annihilation of the Jews of Hungary, was about to begin.

*

Until this last year of the war, Hungary had provided a kind of haven for the Jews of Eastern Europe. The septuagenarian Miklós Horthy, who had served since 1920 as admiral of Hungary's nonexistent navy and as regent for its nonexistent monarchy, joined the war on Hitler's side mainly in order to expand Hungary's rule over the territories to its east. Though anti-Semitism was official Hungarian policy, Jewish businessmen still controlled a large number of Hungarian firms, eleven Jews continued to sit in the Hungarian parliament, and some 130,000 Jews actually served as auxiliary military forces on the Russian front. In contrast to the roundups in Poland, Hungary offered some hope of sanctuary to any fugitive who could slip across its borders, and the Jewish population consequently increased from about 500,000 at the start of the war to more than 800,000 (there were also about 150,000 converted Jews, whose status was disputed according to the conflicting theories of the Nazis and the Catholic Church). They lived in a state of constant fear, but they lived.

By March of 1944, when the Red Army was only a few days' march from the Hungarian border, the Hungarians began talking of surrender. The Nazis' reaction was harsh. Horthy was summoned to a conference in Germany, placed under virtual arrest, and handed an ultimatum: A German plenipotentiary would immediately take charge in Budapest, and German troops would move in to support him. By the time that plenipotentiary arrived at the German Embassy in Budapest on March 19, Adolf Eichmann had already established his headquarters at the Majestic Hotel. The first step, as usual, was to invite the Jewish leaders of Budapest to establish a *Judenrat*, or Jewish Council, that ugly institution by which the Germans assigned the Jews to organize themselves for the execution of orders from Berlin, assigned them to decide for themselves who should be the first to be deported and who should be spared until the next order came. "Do you know what I am?" Eichmann asked at his first meeting with the Jewish Council of Hungary on March 31. "I am a bloodhound."

On May 15, the deportations to Auschwitz began. It was an operation in which Eichmann took considerable pride. In the middle of a major military campaign—in the middle, in fact, of a catastrophic retreat from the battlefields of the east—Eichmann managed to bargain for enough trains to ship half a million Hungarian Jews to their death. There were three trains a day, on the average, each hauling between forty and fifty freight cars, each car carrying about eighty to one hundred people. As on the transports from Germany and France and Holland and everywhere else, the prisoners were given no food or water, but they had been encouraged to bring with them whatever personal possessions might prove valuable in the resettlement camps of the east, and so they embarked with sandwiches and blankets and prayer books and carpets and the family silver and even pouches filled with diamonds, all of it ultimately useless. In less than two months, about 400,000 of these Hungarian Jews found themselves on the ramp at Auschwitz.

"It was ten o'clock one morning that the first of the trains were unloaded," recalled Kitty Hart, a teen-age Polish girl who worked among the mountains of confiscated goods in "Canada." "From the distance we could see masses of people standing, waiting. . . . Their column stretched as far as the eye could see. It seemed as though they were disposing of the whole of Europe. . . ." From the incoming trains, the prospect was ominous. "Peering through a crack in the side of the car . . ." one of the Hungarians, Dr. Miklós Nyiszli, later wrote, "I saw a desertlike terrain: the earth was a yellowish clay . . . broken here and there by a green thicket of trees. Concrete pylons stretched in even rows to the horizon, with barbed wire strung between them from top to bottom. . . . One object immediately caught my eye: an immense square chimney built of red bricks, tapering toward the summit. It towered above a two-story building and looked like a strange factory chimney. I was especially struck by the enormous tongues of flame rising between the lightning rods. . . ." In a less dramatic corner of the camp, Primo Levi noted a basic change: "'Hungarian had become the second language in the camp after Yiddish.'"

Even as the trainloads of Hungarian prisoners began rolling into Auschwitz, the Nazis were exploring a new tactic, not to kill the Jews but to sell them. The idea had been born, apparently, in the first days of the German move into Hungary, when the Wehrmacht discovered two directors of the Manfred Weiss steel empire hiding in a monastery. In exchange for their own freedom to emigrate, along with forty-five of the corporation's chief executives and their relatives, they gave the SS a twenty-five-year lease on the whole empire. Officials in Berlin were fascinated. The ghettos of Poland had offered very few opportunities like this. On April 5, one of the top Nazi officials in Budapest suggested informally to the Jewish leaders an advance deposit of $2 million for the ransom of 100,000 Jews. While this possibility was being explored, Eichmann went a step further. On May 5, just ten days before the first freight cars headed north to Auschwitz, he summoned Joel Brand, a representative of the American-sponsored Joint Distribution Committee, and made what was apparently an official proposal: All the Jews of Hungary could emigrate if the Allies would provide ten thousand heavy military trucks in return. "I was surprised, amazed, happy and confused, all at the same time," Brand testified at Eichmann's trial in Jerusalem. Leaving behind his wife and children as hostages, Brand went to Istanbul on May 19 to establish contact with the British. The Allied answer was harsh but not surprising: No military supplies could be sent to the enemy, no matter what the price might be. Perhaps the Nazis had expected that answer. Even while Brand's hopeless negotiations continued, there was no interruption in the trains to Auschwitz.

On the new ramp at Birkenau, very few selections were made now. The SS men and their dogs herded the prisoners along a cinder path, surrounded by neatly mowed lawns, toward a concrete stairway. A dozen steps led downward to the brightly lit "changing room." Each of these rooms, some three hundred square yards in size, could accommodate as many as one thousand people at a time. There were signs in German, French, Greek and Hungarian, all saying, "Baths and Disinfecting Room." Other signs warned of diseases: "Cleanliness Brings Freedom" and "One Louse Can Kill You." There were wooden benches along the walls, and above these benches there were pegs and coat hangers. More signs told the prisoners to hang up their clothes, and to tie their shoes together by the laces. The pegs were numbered, and the signs told the prisoners to remember their numbers so that they could retrieve their clothes after the baths. Once the prisoners had undressed, they were herded on into another large room, also brightly lit. Once they were all inside, the doors were bolted shut, and the lights were switched off. Some of the prisoners embraced each other as they waited. Some simply waited, numb. The gas had a smell of something burning.

"Twenty minutes later, the electric ventilators were set going in order to evacuate the gas," Dr. Nyiszli later wrote as a medical witness to these scenes. "The doors opened. . . . The bodies were not lying here and there throughout the room but piled in a mass to the ceiling. The reason for this was that the gas first inundated the lower layers of air and rose but slowly toward the ceiling. This forced the victims to trample one another in a frantic effort to escape the gas. . . . I noticed that the bodies of the women, the children and the aged were at the bottom of the pile; at the top, the strongest. Their bodies, which were covered with scratches and bruises from the struggle which had set them against each other, were often interlaced. Blood oozed from their noses and mouths; their faces, bloated and blue, were so deformed as to be almost unrecognizable. . . . The *Sonderkommando* squad, outfitted with large rubber boots, lined up around the hill of bodies and flooded it with powerful jets of water. This was necessary because the final act of those who die by drowning or by gas is an involuntary defecation. Each body was befouled and had to be washed. Once the 'bathing' of the dead was finished . . . they knotted thongs around the wrists . . . and with these thongs they dragged the slippery bodies to the elevators in the next room."

Each crematorium had four large elevators. Each elevator could hold about twenty-five bodies. When it was filled, a bell rang and the elevator rose to the incineration room. Sliding doors opened automatically. The *Sonderkommando* prisoners again seized the thongs around the wrists of the corpses and hauled them onto a chute that carried them

toward the furnaces. One last rite still had to be adminis-
tered. All the victims' hair was shaved off and stored. Then
the Tooth Kommando, eight prisoners who had once been
dental surgeons, set to work. They pried open the corpses'
mouths and yanked out any gold teeth or bridgework they
could find. The gold teeth were dropped into buckets filled
with an acid that burned away all flesh and bone. According
to Dr. Nyiszli's calculations, these operations recovered about
eighteen to twenty pounds of gold per crematorium per day.
The bodies were then loaded onto pushcarts, three to a cart,
and slid into the ovens. The ashes were raked out and loaded
onto trucks and dumped into the Vistula.

Even the most elaborate plans proved insufficient for the
liquidation of the Hungarians that summer. Though the crematoria worked night and day, there were still too many bodies to be destroyed (the highest number actually gassed
within twenty-four hours, Hoess estimated, was nine thousand). The Nazis had to resort once again to the more primitive means that they had previously abandoned. In the fields
of wild flowers that were now blooming behind the crematoria, Hoess ordered nine gigantic pits dug. There he had thousands more bodies dumped in and set afire. It is not easy
to burn bodies, particularly emaciated bodies. The first
attempts, long before the crematoria were built, had used up
a lot of scarce coke. The Nazis had therefore conducted a
series of experiments to find out how to save fuel. They soon
found that if a fat man was burned along with a thin one, the
fat man's fat would serve as fuel to consume the thin one. In
due time, they discovered a still more efficient combination: a
fat man and a thin woman (or vice versa) and a child. By the
time of the slaughter of the Jews of Hungary, they had
reached even higher levels of efficiency. The pits to be filled
with corpses, up to two thousand at a time, had been dug

with slanted bottoms so that the fat could flow into containers and be scooped up and poured back over the burning bodies.

"The corpses in the pit looked as if they had been chained together," according to Filip Müller, a Czech Jew who worked in the *Sonderkommando*. "Tongues of a thousand tiny blue-red flames were licking at them. . . . Blisters which had formed on their skin burst one by one. Almost every corpse was covered with black scorch marks and glistened as if it had been greased. The searing heat had burst open their bellies: There was the violent hissing and sputtering of frying in great heat. . . . Fanned by the wind, the flames, dark red before, now took on a fiery-white hue. . . . The process of incineration took five to six hours. What was left barely filled a third of the pit. The shiny whitish-gray surface was strewn with countless skulls. . . ."

*

While the fires were burning in the summer of 1944—fires that could be seen as far as thirty miles away—the advancing Allied armies finally acquired the ability to destroy the railroad lines from Budapest to Auschwitz, and, for that matter, to destroy Auschwitz itself. Specifically, the U.S. Eighth Air Force based in Britain and the Fifteenth Air Force based in southern Italy were already beginning to bomb military targets in Poland. On April 4, 1944, U.S. reconnaissance planes flying over Auschwitz took some remarkably clear photographs (stowed away in the Pentagon archives until 1979) that show all the essential evidence—the gas chambers and crematoria, the prisoners standing in line—yet even the experts trained to interpret such photographic evidence apparently saw nothing here but a large prison camp.

What was happening at Auschwitz could not be imagined, therefore could not be believed, not even when pho-

tographed, could not be believed even when reported in
detail by escaping prisoners, could not be believed and therefore could not be stopped. There certainly was nothing secret
about the existence of Hitler's concentration camps. The
Nazis almost boasted of them. The very names of Dachau
and Buchenwald, and the reports of terrible things that happened there, served to cow the population. The Final Solution,
however, was officially a state secret, and the SS went to considerable effort to keep it a secret. Even though it was widely
known that deportation to the east meant great hardship and
often death, anyone who spoke of the Auschwitz crematoria
faced severe punishment.

The prisoners tried, at great risk and sacrifice, to tell the
world. As early as November of 1940, a brave Polish officer
named Witold Pilecki, who voluntarily got himself sent to
Auschwitz in order to organize a resistance movement there,
smuggled out a message describing the appalling conditions
at the camp. Appalling conditions are still not the same as
systematic extermination, however. By the summer of 1942,
the Allied capitals had received reports of mass slaughters,
from the camps themselves, from neutral observers, even
from anti-Nazi Germans. The London *Daily Telegraph* reported
that June that more than one million Jews had been killed in
the east. The report was just part of the flood of war news. In
the spring of 1944, finally, Rudolf Vrba and Alfred Weczler
escaped from Auschwitz, reached Czechoslovakia, and produced a sixty-page report on all the details of the gassing and
burning at Birkenau, a report that managed to get to the
White House, the Vatican, the Red Cross, and the Jewish
community leaders in Budapest. Allied leaders remained
doubtful, skeptical, preoccupied with military strategy. There
was a certain amount of anti-Semitism in Washington, and in
the United States at large (not to mention Britain and Russia),

and those who heard the recurrent reports from Poland tended to regard them as propaganda, wildly exaggerated. Even those who were inclined to intervene on behalf of the Jews feared being accused of diverting resources from the overall war effort. As late as November of 1944, just six months before the war ended, Elmer Davis, head of the Office of War Information, tried to suppress a report on Auschwitz out of concern that it would weaken Allied credibility.

In January of 1944, President Roosevelt did establish a War Refugee Board that was supposed to "take all measures within its power to rescue the victims of enemy oppression," but it had very little power to take any such measures. Proposals for military action against the Hungarian deportations attracted little attention or support. One of the first was an open letter by Isaac Rosengarten in the May issue of the magazine *Jewish Forum*, demanding that Budapest be bombed "off the face of the earth." Nobody responded. The War Department issued a statement of policy: "It is not contemplated that units or individuals of the armed forces will be employed for the purpose of rescuing victims of enemy oppression unless such rescues are the direct result of military operations."

In late June, when the killing of the Hungarians had been going on for more than a month, the U.S. legation in Bern reported that both the Jewish deportations and some considerable German troop movements followed five specific railroad lines. "It is urged by all sources of this information . . . " the Bern cable said, "that vital sections of these lines, especially bridges along one, be bombed as the only possible means of slowing down or stopping future deportations." John W. Pehle, executive director of the War Refugee Board, sent a copy of this message to John J. McCloy at the War Department. On July 4, McCloy sent Pehle a message saying that the War Department was opposed to any raid on the railroad lines to Auschwitz: "It could be executed only by the diversion of considerable air support essential to the success of our forces now engaged in decisive operations and would in any case be of such doubtful efficacy that it would not amount to a practical project."

The WRB representative in Bern kept sending Pehle more accounts of the killings. One, apparently the Vrba-Weczler report, provided two eyewitness descriptions of the gas chambers at Birkenau. Pehle's horror presumably reflects Washington's ignorance. "These were the first real verifications we'd had about what was going on in those camps," he later said. With this new evidence, Pehle sent McCloy a more drastic message: "I strongly recommend that the War Department give serious consideration to the possibility of destroying the execution chambers in Birkenau through direct bombing action." McCloy answered simply by passing along a memo prepared by the office of the Chief of Staff, which said once more that such a raid would be an impractical diversion of bombers needed for the war effort. As it happened, U.S. bombers actually did raid Auschwitz in August and again in September, aiming at the synthetic-oil plant affiliated with the camp. They accidentally dropped a few bombs on Auschwitz itself and killed fifteen German soldiers.

Though the Allies refused to strike at the gas chambers of Auschwitz, this was one of the rare occasions when strong words partially made up for the lack of action. The first protest came from the papal nuncio to Budapest, Angelo Rotta, who warned the Hungarian government on the day that the first train left for Auschwitz: "The whole world knows what the deportations mean in practice." The Hungarian bishops complained, too, partly because Eichmann's forces were making no distinctions between Orthodox Jews and those who had converted to Christianity, and finally Monsignor Rotta delivered a gentle protest from Pope Pius XII. The next day, June 25, the aged Admiral Horthy issued instructions that the deportations were to cease. Horthy's authority, particularly over the Germans, was limited. Eichmann's roundups continued. The protests increased. U.S. Secretary of State Cordell Hull delivered a note via the Swiss Legation on June 26 threatening reprisals, and President Roosevelt publicly warned: "Hungary's fate will not be like any other civilization . . . unless deportations are stopped." Sweden sent Raoul Wallenberg as a special envoy to Budapest, authorized to issue thousands of Swedish visas to the threatened Jews, and the Swiss and the Portuguese joined in establishing shelters where Jews could find haven.

Hungary itself stood at the edge of collapse. The Red Army was at its frontiers, and the various authorities in Budapest issued contradictory orders. Premier Dome Sztojay assured the papal nuncio on July 8 that all transports to Auschwitz had stopped. Eichmann still commanded a unit of 150 men, and he sent them to round up another 1,450 Jews on July 14 and pack them aboard a train. An order from Horthy stopped the train before it left Hungary, but two more of Eichmann's trains carried more than 2,000 Jews to Auschwitz on July 19 and 24. They were the last. By now, the Nazi regime itself was crumbling. In the same week that the last transports left Budapest, Count Claus von Stauffenberg planted a bomb next to Hitler at his command post in East Prussia, and for a few hours it seemed as though he had finally rid Germany of its tyrant. Even though most of the July 20 plotters were executed, Hitler's closest lieutenants began wondering how they might save themselves. Himmler had been evacuating prisoners from the Majdanek death camp near Lublin, sending most of them westward to Auschwitz, but a Polish resistance group seized control of Majdanek on July 24 and turned it over to the advancing Russians. Allied war correspondents got their first look at gas chambers, crematoria, canisters of Zyklon B, piles of human bones. Allied broadcasts spoke of atrocities and the prosecution of war criminals, and still Hitler shouted that all Germans would fight on to the death.

At Auschwitz, the halting of the trains from Budapest did not halt the gassings, not yet. The extermination machinery appeared to be running on its own momentum, and the camp was crowded with prisoners, ready to be fed into the machinery. First came the destruction of the so-called Family Camp, the remnant of the prisoners brought from Theresienstadt. This ancient fortress near the Czech-German frontier had originally been a showplace camp, where the Nazis sent distinguished prisoners like Germany's venerable Chief Rabbi Leo Baeck, where they sent decorated Jewish military heroes of the World War, where they sent people who couldn't simply be made to disappear. They and their families, wives, mothers-in-law, lived under prison discipline but under conditions so much better than those in any other prison camp that the Nazis regularly invited in the Red Cross and other international observers to show that the rumors about the concentration camps were greatly exaggerated. Wartime changed all that, however, and thousands of Theresienstadt prisoners were shipped to Auschwitz, where they lived apart, and somewhat better, in the Family Camp.

When the new orders decreed the extermination of the Family Camp, the victims couldn't believe it. They thought that because they had survived so long, they were somehow immune. Even inside the changing room, they shouted their disbelief, "We want to live! We want to work!" The SS men, with their truncheons and their police dogs, herded them toward the gas chambers. "Husbands, helpless themselves, crowded round their wives and children to protect them from blows and also from the savage teeth of the dogs," according to Filip Müller, who was there as one of the *Sonderkommando*. "There was chaos as in the narrow space people pushed and shoved each other, SS men shouted and used their truncheons, and the dogs barked and snapped ferociously. Suddenly a voice began to sing. Others joined in, and the sound swelled into a mighty choir. They sang first the Czechoslovak national anthem and then the Hebrew song 'Hatikvah.' And all this time the SS men never stopped their brutal beatings. It was as if they regarded the singing as a last kind of protest which they were determined to stifle if they could." Four thousand people from the Family Camp were killed on March 9, the last four thousand on July 12.

Hoess turned over his command to Richard Baer on July 29 and returned to Berlin, but the gassing went on. Next came the turn of the gypsies. Himmler had originally rounded them up and sent them to Auschwitz not for extermination but for scientific examination. He had been fascinated for years by the imagery of prehistoric Germany, its Nordic gods and runic inscriptions, its legends of unconquerable Goths and Vandals, and he somehow imagined that the mysterious gypsies were the descendants of these lost tribes. Many of them were shot and beaten in the course of the roundups, but when they finally reached Auschwitz they were isolated and observed and encouraged to carry on their folk traditions. The men were not required to work. A *tzigeuner* orchestra formed, and everybody danced. The women tended the children, and the children clambered all over one another. They too felt themselves immune. Nobody was immune. As that last summer wore on, Himmler lost interest in the gypsies and decreed their annihilation. On the night of August 2, all of them, some four thousand, went to the gas chambers.

*

Himmler himself seemed to have acquired illusions that he could somehow supplant Hitler and negotiate an armistice. He sent envoys to suggest these illusions in neutral Stockholm. He seemed to have denied to himself the fact that Auschwitz would be discovered, and that the discovery would damn him. Very few of the Nazi leaders acted rationally in these last months of the war. Hitler himself rarely emerged from his underground bunker. To the contradictory orders of gassing prisoners or saving them for labor was now added a third policy of moving them from camp to camp, often without food or shelter. While thousands were still being shipped to Auschwitz (one of the very last transports from Holland brought Anne Frank and her family), thousands more were being shipped from Auschwitz back to Germany to work in armaments factories.

At some point during the early fall of 1944—probably between mid-September and mid-October—Himmler decided to end the gassing. It did not end immediately, for the machinery was not easy to stop, but on October 28, when yet another 1,700 Jews from Theresienstadt were crowded into the gas chambers and put to death, they became the last victims of Zyklon B. A trainload of Slovakian Jews who arrived from Bratislava five days later were sent directly to the quarantine camp, with all their luggage. Even this did not mean that the killing had stopped entirely—SS courts still imposed sentences of summary execution, and prisoners still died of starvation and dysentery—but the new edict did mean that the wholesale slaughter had ended. On November 26, an order from Himmler declared: "The crematoria at Auschwitz are to be dismantled . . . "

The prospect of an end to the gassing was terrifying news to one group of prisoners, the *Sonderkommando*. The whole camp swarmed with rumors that everyone in Auschwitz would be killed, but the *Sonderkommando* had always been, as its name indicated, special. Its whole function, its whole existence, depended on the crematoria, and each new squad began by taking part in an essential ritual, the killing of its predecessors. For performing their degrading work in the gas chambers, the men of the *Sonderkommando* were remarkably well treated. They lived in special quarters in the crematoria buildings, and all the plunder of "Canada" was theirs. "The table awaiting us," one of the few survivors later wrote of his arrival at the *Sonderkommando* barracks, "was covered with a heavy silk brocade tablecloth, fine initialed porcelain dishes, and place settings of silver; . . . all sorts of preserves, bacon, jellies, several kinds of salami, cakes and chocolate." They drank fine cognac until they could no longer stand up, and then they fell into bed on linen sheets. Some of the *Sonderkommando* went mad, and some committed suicide, but most of them struggled on for three months or so, and then they ended as they had begun, in a ritual of replacement. Their successors steered them, unprotesting, willing and perhaps even eager to die, into the gas chambers.

The last *Sonderkommando*, however, was not ready to die. The prospect of their imminent annihilation in the last days of the camp suddenly filled them with a passion to rebel. They turned to the Polish underground for help, but the prospect of the end of Auschwitz, the same prospect that inspired the *Sonderkommando* to rebellion, inspired the Polish underground to caution. To some extent, the Polish underground always emphasized caution. Its primary goal was to organize and defend itself, and to that end its agents maneuvered themselves into relatively safe positions in the hospital and the administrative offices. Open rebellion remained a distant possibility. In the view of the underground leaders, these self-protective maneuvers justified themselves as a matter of survival, and, as the Soviet Army drew nearer to Auschwitz, survival seemed all the more to require that everyone lie low.

The last *Sonderkommando* had been expanded, in order to deal with the Hungarians, from about two hundred to seven hundred men, a fairly formidable force, and as these men realized that they themselves were doomed they began to arm. By theft and bribery, and with infinite stealth, they smuggled into their luxurious quarters, one by one, a pistol, then a grenade, then more grenades. As early as June, the *Sonderkommando* planned a full-scale uprising. The prisoners would attack their SS guards, seize their weapons and uniforms, then bluff their way past the sentries, escape into the woods and join forces with Polish partisan units. But the Polish underground kept warning that it was too early, too dangerous. Then the SS men began to sense trouble. One of the ringleaders of the *Sonderkommando*, a *Kapo* named Kamiński, who was in charge of Crematorium II, was suddenly arrested, tortured, and shot. The other rebel leaders turned cautious.

On October 7, the Polish underground agents in the Auschwitz administrative office sent word to the *Sonderkommando* that the SS had decided on their liquidation, and that it might come at any moment. The ringleaders gathered inside Crematorium IV to decide what to do. That same day, an SS officer named Busch had told the *Kapo*s of Crematorium IV that he needed three hundred men from the *Sonderkommando* to go and clear rubble in a town in Upper Silesia. The *Kapo*s suspected that this was a ruse that would lead to their death. Filip Müller, who was one of the prisoners standing at roll call in the yard, noted that some prisoners didn't answer when their numbers were called. Busch sent several guards into the crematorium to look for them. "The guards were just leaving," Müller recalled, "when quite suddenly from out of the ranks of selected prisoners they were pelted with a hail of stones. Some SS men were wounded, but others managed to dodge the stones and were drawing their guns and starting to shoot wildly into the crowd of prisoners. Two more SS men had managed to get away to the camp street, where they grabbed two bicycles leaning against the camouflage fence and sped off . . . "

Inside the crematorium itself, the assembled ringleaders had been surprised by a *Kapo* who was not in on the plot, and so they killed him. Then they packed the hated crematorium with their precious store of explosives, and some oil-soaked rags, and blew it up. "I saw the red-tiled roof and supporting beams of [the] crematorium blow off," Dr. Nyiszli recalled, "followed by an immense spiral of flame and black smoke. No sooner than a minute later, machine-gun fire broke out. . . . The dismal wail of sirens began. . . . From the window I saw eighty to one hundred trucks arriving. The first one pulled up in front of our crematorium. Half a company jumped out and formed up in battle formation in front of the barbed-wire fences. . . . The *Sonderkommando* men . . . were spraying the SS troops with bullets and grenades. . . . I saw several soldiers drop, either dead or wounded. Seeing this, the besiegers . . . brought up fifty well-trained police dogs and unleashed them. . . ."

The explosion in Crematorium IV signaled the *Sonderkommando* in the other installations that the revolt had begun. In Crematorium II, the rebels quickly seized control. They threw one SS man and one German *Kapo* into the furnace and burned them alive. They also beat one German soldier to death. Then they poured out into the prison yard, cut holes in the surrounding fence, and fled toward the woods. But they ran in the wrong direction, not northeast toward the Vistula but southwest toward the Rajsko subcamp. That kept them within the confines of the camp's outer fences.

In fact, the *Sonderkommando* did almost everything wrong. The uprising had originally been planned for the night but started in broad daylight. All the crematoria were supposed to rebel at once, and in silence, so that the rebels could secretly organize a mass escape, but the shooting at Crematorium IV warned the SS men of trouble, and they quickly secured the other crematoria. And since the uprising had not been coordinated with the Polish underground, there were no partisan units to help anyone who escaped.

"Prisoners were now milling about aimlessly and panic-stricken while from all sides they were met by a shower of bullets," according to Müller's account of the pandemonium in the yard of Crematorium IV. "One by one they fell to the ground fatally injured. Finally a large number raced toward the barbed wire to try and break through." Müller decided on a different course. He sought refuge inside the ruins. "The crematorium was still burning fiercely. The wooden doors were ablaze, several of the wooden beams were charred and dangling from the ceiling, and there was a fire raging in the coke store. The windows on the opposite wall were riddled with bullet holes. Outside, the firing continued. . . . In a flash I remembered a place where I would be safe from bullets: inside the flue leading from the ovens to the chimney. I lifted one of the cast-iron covers, climbed down and closed the cover behind me. . . . As I glanced up I glimpsed, framed by the four soot-blackened chimney walls, a small square of deep-blue sky. . . ."

Outside, the sound of machine gun fire slowly died down. That was because the truckloads of SS men had surrounded the woods where the prisoners had fled, and now they were slowly closing in. Other SS men with dogs headed southward in pursuit of the prisoners who had escaped from Crematorium II. They trapped most of them in a barn near Rajsko. Partly out of caution, partly for sport, the SS men did not attack the barn but set fire to it. As the prisoners fled the flames, the SS men shot them down.

When the shooting was over, the SS men brought all the corpses back to the yard outside Crematorium IV. They counted some 250 of them, but when they checked their lists and records they found that twelve of the *Sonderkommando* were missing. They were about to set out in search of them when the air-raid sirens began sounding. That forced a halt to the search, for everyone was supposed to take cover. Before they did so, the SS men rounded up every prisoner they could find from the *Sonderkommando* in Crematoria II and IV. They forced them to their knees, then shot them, about two hundred men in all. When the all-clear finally sounded at sundown, the SS men and their dogs started their search for the twelve missing prisoners. They trapped them in a building on the far side of the Vistula, where they had taken refuge for the night. The SS men shot them all and then dragged their bodies back to be piled up next to the corpses lying outside Crematorium IV. The SS casualties: three dead, 12 wounded.

After the revolt, the remnants of the *Sonderkommando* consisted of 198 men, who still hoped that they could somehow survive. The SS had other plans. At about two in the afternoon of November 17, they were all marched to Crematorium II, and the doors were locked behind them. They were not ordered to undress, for there was no need for any pretense of showers. They all knew they were going to die, and they attempted neither protest nor revolt. As they stood silently awaiting their execution, they suddenly heard the voice of a man whom they knew only as "the dayyan" (judge). He was a thin, bespectacled Pole of about thirty, who devoted himself to the study of Scripture. The Nazis often amused themselves by assigning such people to the most degrading work in the camp, particularly the latrine-cleaning detail known as the *Scheisskommando*, but this dayyan, assigned to the crematoria, absolutely refused to take any part in the mutilation and burning of the corpses. He also rejected the luxuries of the *Sonderkommando*, eating only the bread rations of the ordinary prisoners. Such insubordination should have led quickly to his execution, but there was something about this unworldly dayyan that prompted the Nazis to spare him. He was assigned to a detail that sorted out the hair shaved from the dead, and even here he spent his time arguing with prisoners who raged at the God who had consigned them to such a fate. "Listen, Dayyan, not once have I felt even a breath of divine justice here," one twenty-year-old youth named Menachem charged. "Absolutely everything that you stuffed into my head in school is just nonsense. There is no God, and if there is one, he is an ox and a bastard!" The SS men guffawed at such disputation, according to Müller, who recorded this one, but the dayyan did his best to uphold the faith even in these disastrous circumstances. "If the Haggadah commands man in each generation to look at himself as if he himself had migrated from Egypt," he said, "the brothers who perhaps by a miracle will manage to survive will read the Haggadah, made whole by their experiences in Auschwitz."

Now, sealed into their underground tomb, the last *Sonderkommando* heard once again the voice of the dayyan.

"Brothers!" he called out. "Fellow Jews . . . Fate has allotted us the cruelest of tasks, that of participating in our own destruction, of witnessing our own disappearance, down to the very ashes to which we are reduced. . . . We must accept, resignedly, as sons of Israel should, that this is the way things must be. God has so ordained it. Why? It is not for us, miserable humans, to seek the answer. This is the fate that has befallen us. Do not be afraid of death. What is life worth, even if, by some strange miracle, we should manage to remain alive? We would return to our cities and towns to find cold and pillaged homes. . . . We would wander like the restless, shuffling shadows of our former selves, of our completed pasts, finding nowhere any peace or rest."

A few minutes after this impassioned sermon in the underground mausoleum, three SS men with machine guns opened the door and ordered all doctors to return to their quarters to await further assignment, and that was how Dr. Nyiszli, one of three doctors who emerged into the sunlight, survived to record this scene. The next time he saw the last *Sonderkommando*, they were charred beyond recognition. The SS had taken them all out into the fields outside the camp and turned flame-throwers on them.

This was part of Himmler's deluded attempt to destroy all the evidence of what had happened at Auschwitz and the other Polish death camps. Once Himmler had ordered that the crematoria were to be dismantled, teams of prisoners happily began taking apart Crematoria II and III, but, just like the building of those installations, the dismantling took time. One set of furnaces was kept burning to deal with the camp's routine deaths and with the destruction of papers (and one of the SS men, who liked to raise rabbits, kept several of his hutches in an unused gas chamber). The Auschwitz authorities seemed confused about how to start the obliteration of evidence. Clerks began going through the voluminous files that had so carefully been kept for so long—the official police dossiers on thousands of interrogations, the carefully falsified

death certificates on hundreds of thousands of killings—trying
to decide what was incriminating, what should be burned
and what should be saved. First they burned the lists of those
incoming prisoners who had gone directly from the railroad
ramp to the gas chambers, and then the files of the Political
Department, and then the hospital records of the thousands
who had been murdered by phenol injections. Then came the
great sorting out of "Canada." Carloads of clothes and furniture and jewelry and musical instruments were shipped to
Berlin, carloads more were judged worthless and consigned
to the flames. And then the crematorium equipment. Details
of prisoners worked all through December, through
Christmas, to dismantle the furnaces and pack the supplies
for shipment to Mauthausen and Gross-Rosen. And finally
the funeral pits. Squads of prisoners dug them up, sifted out
the bones and ashes to be dumped in the Vistula, then
replanted the desecrated earth with grass.

*

The last spasms of killing were relentlessly legal. On
January 6, 1945, when the camp was covered with a heavy
blanket of snow, the prisoners in the women's camp at
Birkenau were assembled to watch a hanging. The SS had
been working for three months to discover who had provided the explosives used in the revolt of the *Sonderkommando*, and after subjecting certain suspects to torture they
had identified four young Jewish women who worked at I. G.
Farben's Union munitions factory. These four were thereupon
convicted of smuggling and sentenced to death. Two of them
were marched up to a specially erected gallows. "They were
wearing their regular clothes, except that they did not have
their coats on," recalled Judith Sternberg Newman, an eyewitness and a good friend of one of the victims, Aline
Gärtner. "They walked calmly, their faces composed. . . . An

SS man bound their hands behind their backs. . . . Aline was then pulled up on the table, and her last words were, 'You'll pay for this. I shall die now, but your turn will come soon.' The executioner fixed the noose around her neck, and she was pulled up by the rope. Now a noose was put around the other girl's neck. . . . All she said when they lifted her up on the table was, 'I hope all my comrades will get their freedom.' They hung there like two marionettes, turning in the breeze. It was a horrible sight."

The second woman, a Pole, had a younger sister who was also among the condemned, but her hanging had been delayed. "She had been left behind in her block, for she had suffered a complete nervous breakdown," Mrs. Newman reported. "Her wild screams could be heard from afar." The execution was not delayed for long. Just after dark, that same night, the mad woman and the fourth condemned prisoner were both taken out to the gallows and hanged. Those were the last official executions at Auschwitz.

*

The Soviet Army, which had been stalled for weeks within about fifty miles of Auschwitz, finally launched a surprise offensive on January 12, 1945. Within a week, its artillery was pounding the outskirts of the camp, and shortly after midnight of January 18 the Nazis ordered a general evacuation. They dynamited the brick walls of Crematorium V, the last one still standing. They set fire to "Canada." It was about ten degrees below zero when the SS began routing the ragged prisoners out onto the snow-covered fields and bullying them into the customary ranks of five. Even then, there were long delays, roll calls, shouts and confusion. Several thousand prisoners in the camp hospital argued about whether to join the evacuation, and those who wanted to flee fought over the few pairs of wooden clogs that the authorities had left them to use in going to the latrines. Among the SS too there were arguments about whether to kill everyone who couldn't march. There had been various plans drawn up for the complete annihilation of the camp and all remaining prisoners, but nobody had ever formally issued the orders to carry out this final massacre. By now, the SS men were thinking mainly of flight from the dreaded Russians, so they decided simply to leave the sick and injured behind. Or perhaps no one decided anything, and the sick were just abandoned in the chaos of the four-day evacuation.

"Order and discipline had disappeared," Olga Lengyel recalled of her last round through the hospital wards. "Most of the sick had left their beds and were massing around the stove in the middle of the room." Several patients had broken into the supervisor's quarters and stolen some food, and now they were frying *plazki* on the stove. Mrs. Lengyel led a band of patients in attacking the hospital storehouse with pickaxes; inside, they seized a large supply of bread. When she had wrapped up her few possessions in a blanket roll that she knotted at both ends, she joined the stream of prisoners heading out into the snowy night.

"Thirty guards stood at the gate," she reported. "Before letting us out, they examined us one by one under a pocket flashlight, in what became another selection. Those who were judged to be too old or too feeble were driven back into the camp. Once we were outside the camp, we had to line up, as always, in columns of five. A new period of waiting began. This lasted for about two hours, for the whole convoy was to consist of six thousand women. Then the SS closed the gates. An order was barked. Our column was under way. . . . After we had traveled some distance, we came to a turn in the road. Here we looked back for our last glimpse of Birkenau. . . . Everything was plunged into darkness; and only burning embers, where the crematory records were being incinerated, feebly lighted the barracks and the barbed-wire fences."

Dr. Nyiszli, who had gone to bed early in a room near the crematoria, was wakened shortly after midnight by machine-gun fire and flashes of light and the thud of footsteps running past his door. He prudently outfitted himself with a warm overcoat, a two-pound can of food, even some cigarettes, and as he left his barracks he passed the room where the gold torn from the prisoners' teeth was stored. "We did not even think of stopping to take some of it. What was money when one's life was at stake? We had learned that nothing lasts and that no value is absolute."

Nyiszli simply walked unchallenged through the main gate, past the deserted ramp where all the doomed transports had come to a halt. Outside the firelit Birkenau gate, he saw a crowd of about three thousand prisoners waiting docilely for the SS to tell them what to do. He decided to join this crowd in the hope that their numbers would provide him some security during the flight to the west. At about 1 A.M. the last SS man left Birkenau. "He closed the iron gates and cut off the lights from the main switchboard, which was located near the entrance. . . . Birkenau sank into darkness." Even as the prisoners started their march, a Russian advance guard opened fire. "They were using submachine guns and had the support of a light tank," Nyiszli reported. "The SS returned the fire and shouted for us to take cover on the ground. The fire was heavy on both sides. Then, in a little while, all grew quiet again and we resumed our journey across the sterile, snow-covered earth of Silesia."

Behind them, they left a macabre simulacrum of the great death camp, inhabited now only by a regiment of the dying. "The Lager, hardly dead, had already begun to decompose," wrote Primo Levi, confined to the infectious ward with scarlet fever. "No more water, or electricity, broken windows and doors slamming to in the wind, loose . . . roofs screeching, ashes from the fire drifting high, afar. The work of the bombs [from a recent air raid] had been completed by the work of man: ragged, decrepit, skeleton-like patients at all able to move dragged themselves everywhere on the frozen soil, like an invasion of worms. They had ransacked all the empty huts in search of food and wood. . . ."

To be leaving Birkenau under any circumstances seemed a kind of liberation, but this trek to the west was to be cruel. The sixty thousand prisoners who were marched off into the snow and darkness had been issued only one day's ration of bread. Most of them had no coats or blankets. They were heading vaguely toward the Gross-Rosen camp, some 150 miles to the west, but most of the prisoners did not know where they were going, and many of their guards did not know how to get there. "An icy wind blew in violent gusts," according to the narrator of Elie Wiesel's *Night*. "But we marched without faltering. The SS made us increase our pace. 'Faster, you swine, you filthy sons of bitches . . . ' We were no longer marching; we were running. Like automatons. The SS were running, too, their weapons in their hands. We looked as though we were fleeing before them. Pitch darkness. Every now and then, an explosion in the night. They had orders to fire on any who could not keep up. . . . I repeated to myself, 'Don't think. Don't stop. Run.' Near me, men were collapsing in the dirty snow. Shots . . . "

As the first dawn broke, Dr. Nyiszli's unit had gone about ten miles from Auschwitz. "All along the way I noticed pots and blankets and wooden shoes that had been abandoned by a convoy of women who had preceded us. A few miles farther on we came upon a much sadder sight: every forty or fifty yards, a bloody body lay in a ditch beside the road. For miles and miles it was the same story: bodies everywhere. Exhausted, they had been unable to walk any farther; when they had strayed from the ranks an SS man had dispatched them with a bullet in the back."

In the opposite direction came, of all people, Rudolf Hoess, the creator of Auschwitz, now frantic and enraged at this spectacle of disorderly flight. Driving eastward from his headquarters in Berlin, he had stopped at Gross-Rosen, where he found his successor, Baer, bumbling around in an effort to make what Hoess called "preparations for the reception of the prisoners." Of the prisoners themselves, Baer seemed to know very little. "He had no idea where his camp might be wandering," Hoess reported.

Hoess climbed back into his car and drove eastward. His main purpose was to check on "the order for the destruction of everything important." The carrying out of every order was important to Hoess, of course, but this particular order for the burning of evidence was one that he hoped might ultimately save him from the hangman. "I was only able to get as far as the Oder, near Ratibor," Hoess wrote, "for the Russian armored spearheads were already fanning out on the far side of that river. On all the roads and tracks in Upper Silesia west of the Oder I now met columns of prisoners, struggling through the deep snow. They had no food. Most of the noncommissioned officers in charge of these stumbling columns of corpses had no idea where they were supposed to be going. They only knew that their final destination was Gross-Rosen. But how to get there was a mystery."

Since Himmler had by now issued orders against the wanton killing of prisoners, Hoess claimed that he too "gave strict orders to the men in charge of all these columns that they were not to shoot prisoners incapable of further marching." He found the new orders ignored. "On the road near

Leobschütz," he said, "I constantly came upon the bodies of
prisoners who had just been shot, and which were therefore
still bleeding. On one occasion, as I stopped my car by a dead
body, I heard revolver shots quite near. I ran toward the
sound, and saw a soldier in the act of stopping his motorcycle
and shooting a prisoner leaning against a tree. I shouted at
him, asking him what he thought he was doing, and what
harm the prisoner had done him. He laughed impertinently
in my face, and asked me what I proposed to do about it. I
drew my pistol and shot him forthwith. He was a sergeant
major in the Air Force."

Tramping through the snow, famished and exhausted, the
prisoners clung to the idea that they would eventually reach
a railroad line that would carry them to the west. Those who
actually survived long enough to reach such a lifeline soon
discovered, once again, still further ordeals ahead. Sim
Kessel, the French boxer, who was now missing a finger,
marched for a week before reaching a switching yard, and
there the SS troops clubbed the prisoners onto a string of
open-topped freight cars. Kessel was one of seventy. "We
were forced to lie down, one on top of another, all tangled
and mixed together . . . ," he recalled. "Not a hair showed
above the edge. The SS guaranteed this by firing machine
guns over our heads. . . . For five days we lay there almost
motionless and without as much as a crust, or a drop of
water. . . . In the terrible cold many of the inert bodies slowly
gave up what remained of life in them. . . . I spent the last
two days in an on-again-off-again coma. Noticing that my
two nearest neighbors were dead, I took their blankets and
then snuggled under their stiff bodies for warmth. On the
evening of the fifth day we reached Mauthausen. We were
ordered to get off the freight car, and I was strong enough to

get down. In the few minutes we waited on the platform, I tried to count the men who had survived and could still walk. There were nine of us."

Far to the east, the grim and partly gutted ruins of Auschwitz lay abandoned in the snow. At 3 P.M. on January 27, 1945, more than a week after the SS evacuation, some white-caped reconnaissance scouts of the First Ukrainian Front emerged from the woods and saw the rows and rows of barracks, the miles of barbed wire, the empty guardposts. Inside the camp, they found some 7,650* of those half-dead prisoners whom the SS had judged too feeble to be worth evacuating. "There was a mad rush to shake them by the hand and shout out our gratitude," one of the survivors, Karel Ornstein, said of the liberators. "Several prisoners waved red scarves. The shouts of joy [could] have gone on forever. . . ."

Of those last sixty thousand prisoners who marched west from Auschwitz, about one third died along the way. And for the survivors, survival meant to arrive, starving and frozen and exhausted, at some new destination like Mauthausen, a hilltop fortress near Linz where tens of thousands of prisoners had been worked to death in the nearby granite quarries. Yet, in a way, the 8,365 Auschwitz prisoners who reached Mauthausen were lucky. Most of them got some food and new clothing and then were shipped to

---

* This number, like so many Auschwitz statistics, is hardly more than an official approximation. Indeed, the total number of Auschwitz survivors is almost as cloudy as the number of dead. The estimates generally run around 30,000. The essential fact in all these estimates is that of all the prisoners shipped to Auschwitz, fewer than 1% survived.

smaller camps in the area. A far worse fate awaited the
largest contingent, perhaps ten thousand in all, which finally
arrived at Bergen-Belsen.

*

Bergen-Belsen, near the old Hanseatic town of Hannover,
was once a Wehrmacht camp for wounded prisoners of war.
It was quite small, designed for seven thousand men, who
lived in a series of neat little buildings connected by neat little pathways. Not until 1943 did the SS get control of half the
camp, and even then it remained a relatively "model" camp.
Many of the prisoners confined here were rich or eminent
Jews whom the SS hoped to ransom in one way or another.
As the war drew to an end, however, Bergen-Belsen was first
crowded, then swamped, then engulfed by the hordes streaming westward from the slave camps of Poland.

First came the SS men themselves, notably Captain Josef
Kramer. A brutal professional who had served in the SS since
1932, Kramer had gone with Hoess in 1940 to join in the
building of Auschwitz and had been made commandant of
Birkenau in the spring of 1944 to preside over the gassing of
the Hungarians. He was a heavyset man, with large ears and
crew-cut brown hair and an aloof manner that one prisoner
described as his "Buddhalike air." Dr. Lingens, however,
remembered once seeing him in a rage, "his bull neck low-
ered, his thick head and jowls purple." This was the man
who brought to Bergen-Belsen in December of 1944 the
harshest Auschwitz methods. "We had suddenly the feeling
that Belsen was going to become a second Auschwitz," a
prisoner named Ada Bimke testified when Kramer and forty-
four other Belsen officials came before a British military court
at Lüneburg in the autumn of 1945. "They started with roll
calls, *Appelle*, and those SS men who previously did not hit

the prisoners started now to do so. . . . I worked in the hospital at Belsen, and many prisoners were admitted suffering from beating."

Like Hoess at Auschwitz, Kramer found himself flooded with new prisoners, but, unlike Hoess, he was not supposed to gas them. He protested to Berlin that he had no room, no food, no supplies, and yet the transports from the East kept streaming in, a grotesque reversal of the transports from the West that Kramer had once received at Birkenau. In the week of April 4–13 alone, 28,000 new prisoners arrived. Kramer hardly even attempted to combat the impending famine but simply accepted it as some incomprehensible and unavoidable vagary of war. "It was hardly possible to get any potatoes or vegetables," he testified at the Lüneburg trial, "and although I had been getting bread from Celle and Hannover the air raids destroyed part of the bakeries and the road and rail system. It was when the air raids started that, for the first time, bread did not arrive in the camp. . . . At last I lost patience, and told them [the authorities in Hannover], through my administrative officials, that if I did not get any potatoes or vegetables sent I would hold them responsible for any sort of catastrophe which might happen." In actual fact, Kramer knew that there was a Wehrmacht training school just two miles away which had eight hundred tons of food and a bakery capable of producing sixty thousand loaves of bread a day, but Kramer did not ask for help, he testified, because that would have required "special papers." And so the catastrophe happened.

Guns and clubs can kill people, but nothing is more lethal than simply keeping fifty thousand prisoners confined behind barbed wire with no food, almost no water, and just a few latrines. Within a few weeks, typhus and dysentery were everywhere, and so were the rats. The famished prisoners, who knew the war was almost over, ambled about or sat in a stupor, waiting for someone to rescue them. "There was no bread for four weeks before the arrival of the British troops," an Auschwitz prisoner named Dora Szafran testified at the Lüneburg trial. "During the whole time I was at Belsen, people were not taken for baths nor were their clothes changed. Toward morning there were several hundred corpses in the blocks and around the blocks. When the commandant . . . came along to inspect people, the corpses were cleared away from the front of the blocks, but inside they were full of corpses." Some of the survivors even resorted to cannibalism. "I actually saw a prisoner whip out a knife," Harold Le Druillenec testified, "cut a portion out of the leg of a dead body, and quickly put it in his mouth, naturally frightened of being seen in the act of doing so."

The first man from the outside world to enter this inferno was a British psychological-warfare officer named Captain Derek Sington, who had been ordered to negotiate the takeover of the camp. He could hardly believe what he saw. Along with 28,000 women and 12,000 men, all haggard and emaciated, there were about 13,000 unburied corpses, some stacked in piles like pieces of firewood, many just lying around wherever they had fallen. (Among the dead was Anne Frank, who succumbed here during the last weeks of the war.) The half-mad Commandant Kramer proved to be "genial and friendly," said Sington. He described his prisoners to the British as "habitual criminals, felons, and homosexuals." He accompanied Sington on a tour of the camp in a British armored car, and the British repeatedly announced through bullhorns that the camp was now liberated. The prisoners could hardly believe what they saw. Many of them simply stared numbly at their liberators. Some of the women began sobbing. A few ceremoniously scattered twigs and leaves in the path of the armored car. Kramer became alarmed. "Now the tumult is beginning," he said to Sington. The orderly camp had been "disrupted." Behind him, Sington heard the sound of gunfire as the Germans attempted even after their surrender to enforce their authority. Sington strode up to a Wehrmacht officer who was firing just over the heads of some prisoners and ordered him at gunpoint to stop. Sington then told Kramer that if any prisoners were shot for any reason whatever, the British would immediately shoot an equal number of SS men. The SS grudgingly acquiesced.

"Feed the living and bury the dead," the Marquis of Pombal had proposed as his prescription for healing the ravages of the Lisbon earthquake in 1755. The British did just that. As gently as soldiers can, they fed and cared for the starving prisoners and brought most of them back to life. Many of them, however, were beyond all help. An estimated ten thousand inmates liberated at Bergen-Belsen died shortly after their liberation. As for the mountains of decaying corpses, the British simply brought in bulldozers and pushed the bodies into vast pits and then covered them with lime. Then they bulldozed the rest of the camp, everything. All that remains of Bergen-Belsen today is a series of swollen graves, covered with grass.

*

Auschwitz remains. It is a museum now, and the marshy grass grows tall alongside the rusting railroad tracks that end at the haunted ramp of Birkenau. The Poles wanted to keep everything just as it was—"a monument of the martyrdom of the Polish nation," according to the official decree, "and of other nations"—and so they left the giant brick crematoria in ruins, just as the SS men had left them in their frenzy to escape. At the same time, the Poles wanted to preserve and demonstrate and explain, and so they repaired and repainted some of the grimmest barracks and filled them with educational exhibitions.

Here in Block 4 is a "hall of nations," outfitted with the flags of all the occupied lands that gave up their citizens to Auschwitz. And here an artfully constructed model of the destroyed gas chambers, and here a mountain of the hair cut from the women who were murdered. The Soviet troops who liberated Auschwitz found more than fifteen thousand pounds of this hair awaiting shipment back to Germany. And here in Block 5 is a display case containing all the artificial arms and legs, dozens and dozens of them, that were stripped from crippled prisoners before their execution. Here in Block 6 is another glass case in which the tattered rags of the prisoners are neatly hung up for observation, like the costumes of a tribe that has long since vanished. And here, forever preserved, is the daily food ration that so many prisoners never got, the bowl of soup, the chunk of bread, the dab of margarine, the shriveled slice of sausage. Here in Block 7 are the three-tiered bunks, all neat and clean now, and empty.

In the cellar of Block 11 the "standing cells" are available for inspection, and the benches on which prisoners were flogged, and the clubs that were used to flog them. And here, next to the camp kitchen, is the long wooden gallows, where Rudolf Hoess, having confessed and testified and explained, was brought back to be hanged. "I too must now be destroyed," he had written. "The world demands it." And at Birkenau, finally, a rough stone pathway leads past the series of plaques that attempted to commemorate the dead: "Four million people suffered and died here at the hands of the Nazi murderers between the years 1940 and 1945."*

It is a great place for wreaths, for official visits by states-men bearing wreaths. They pause to write worthy sentiments in the official visitors' book. West German Foreign Minister Walter Scheel, who was a Luftwaffe navigator during World War II, was the first German cabinet minister to make the pil-grimage and deposit a wreath. "It will be our task to preserve these highest values—dignity of man, peace among people," he wrote in the visitors' book. Gerald Ford was the first American President to come, and two U.S. Marines deposited his wreath of red and white carnations. "This monument . . . " he wrote in the official book, "inspires us further to the dedi-cated pursuit of peace, cooperation and security for all peo-ples."

And the first Polish Pope, John Paul II, who was studying in his seminary during most of the Auschwitz years, arrived at the camp by means of a white helicopter and then a limou-sine, its path strewn with flowers. He fell to his knees in prayer. "Peace!" he cried. "Only peace! Only peace!" The carefully preserved barbed wire was strung with TV cables that day, and some of the reporters on the scene were impressed by other peculiarities. "It was a day of pitiless

---

* In 1990, the Auschwitz authorities responded to Jewish complaints by chis-eling away the message on the plaques and asking the International Auschwitz Council to devise a satisfactory new one. After two years of con-sultations, the Council worked out a text that says: "About one and a half million men, women, children and infants, mainly Jews from different coun-tries of Europe, were murdered here. The world was silent." Not wanting to leave anybody out, it also pays tribute to the "Jews, Poles, Gypsies, Soviet prisoners of war, and others who suffered . . . " adding a quote from Job: "O Earth, cover not up my blood/And let my cry never cease."

heat," recalled one of them, Neal Ascherson. "The Polish crowds poured into the vast Birkenau enclosures hour after hour, buying Catholic souvenirs, memorial postcards, soft drinks, and chocolate from the stalls set up along the way. . . . The Papal dais stood astride the blackened rails which led to the ramp. . . . Much had given way to time and nature since my last visit. Stout trees had grown out of soil composed of what had been human ash. . . . The poplars planted by the Nazis to screen the crematoria have grown enormously tall and graceful, stirring their tips against the blue sky. . . ."

The Polish purpose in all this commemoration is to make sure that the world remembers what happened at Auschwitz, and that it learns the lesson of what happened. To Polish officialdom—Józef Cyrankiewicz, who became premier in 1947, had been a prisoner at Auschwitz from 1941 to 1945—what happened and what it meant appeared perfectly clear. That was evident in the plaque mourning "the martyrdom of the Polish nation" and warning against "international fascism."

To others, neither the meaning of the event nor the lesson to be learned from it is quite so obvious. None of us can approach Auschwitz—neither the museum standing in the ruins nor the very idea of the great death camp on the Vistula—without all the intellectual and spiritual burdens that we carry with us. We see Auschwitz and we judge Auschwitz according to the way we see and judge the human race, and life, and God.

Auschwitz was a world unlike any other because it was created and governed according to the principles of absolute evil. Its only function was death. The first question, then, is whether we see Auschwitz as the epitome of life itself, an incarnation of the darkest principles of Machiavelli and Hobbes, or whether we see it as a mirror image of the true life, a Satanic perversion of some divine plan that we have not yet discovered. From that central enigma flow all the lesser contradictions that still bedevil anyone who seeks to understand the mystery of Auschwitz. Did it represent the ultimate evil of the German nation, and was that the evil of German rationality or of German irrationality? Or did it represent, conversely, the apotheosis of Jewish suffering? And was that suffering simply the result of centuries of anti-Semitism, or was it part of the fulfillment of the prophecy that the tormented Jews would someday return to Palestine, return, as Ezekiel had written, to "the land that is restored from the ravages of the sword, where people are gathered out of many nations upon the mountains of Israel"?

It can be argued that Auschwitz proves there is no God, neither for the Jews nor for the Catholics, neither for atheists nor for Jehovah's Witnesses, who all went equally helpless to their death. "If all this was possible," wrote one Hungarian survivor, Eugene Heimler, "if men could be herded like beasts toward annihilation, then all that I had believed in before must have been a lie. There was not, there could not be, a God, for he could not condone such godlessness." But such declarations have been made at every moment of extreme crisis by those who see God only in success and happiness. Since all efforts to prove or explain God's purposes demonstrate only the futile diligence of worker ants attempting to prove the existence of Mozart, Auschwitz can just as well prove a merciful God, an indifferent God, or, perhaps best, an unknowable God. William Styron, in *Sophie's Choice*, suggested the answer as a riddle: "At Auschwitz, tell me, where was God?" The answer is only another question: "Where was man?"

The evidence of Auschwitz has demonstrated many things about humanity. It has demonstrated that men (and women too) are capable of committing every evil the mind can conceive, that there is no natural or unwritten law that says of any atrocity whatever: This shall not be done. It has demonstrated that men can also bear and accept every evil, and that they will do so in order to survive. To survive, even just from one day to the next, they will kill and let kill, they will rob and betray their friends, steal food rations from the dying, inform on neighbors, do anything at all, just for one more day. The evidence of Auschwitz has demonstrated just as conclusively that men will sacrifice themselves for others, sometimes quite selflessly. Franciszek Gajnowiczek, for example, is a stooped, gray-haired man, who has survived Auschwitz to testify that when he was selected at random for execution one day in 1941, a Franciscan priest named Maximilian Kolbe stepped forward and volunteered to take his place, and did take his place and did die. (The Vatican in due time proclaimed Kolbe to be beatified and well on the way to sainthood.) The evidence has demonstrated, more-over, that those who are ready to sacrifice themselves for one another, those who share a commitment to some political or spiritual purpose, are at least as likely to survive as those who make survival their only goal. The evidence, in other words, is as contradictory as human nature itself. "The truth about Auschwitz?" Józef Cyrankiewicz once reflected. "There is no person who could tell the whole truth about Auschwitz."

Elie Wiesel, who was sent to Auschwitz as a boy, remembered the place as hellish, and when he finally revisited it in 1979 he was overwhelmed by its beauty. "The low clouds, the dense forest, the calm solemnity of the scenery," he wrote. "The silence is peaceful, soothing. Dante understood nothing. Hell is a setting whose serene splendor takes the breath away." When Wiesel tried to decipher the meaning of that serene graveyard, he was helpless. "How was it possible?" he wrote. "We shall never understand. Even if we manage some-how to learn every aspect of that insane project, we will never understand it. . . . I think I must have read all the books— memoirs, documents, scholarly essays and testimonies writ-ten on the subject. I understand it less and less." That is the survivor's message on the mystery of survival, but the name-less dayyan may have been preaching a richer variation of the same message when he urged the men of the last *Sonderkommando* not to be afraid as they waited in the under-ground chamber for the fulfillment of God's incomprehensi-ble will.

A Note on Sources

Much of what happened at Auschwitz remains somewhat mysterious, for many of the Nazi records were falsified with terms like "special handling," and many of even these falsified records were destroyed in the evacuation of the camp. The most valuable source of information is the testimony of the prisoners who were there, who have done their best to bear witness to what they experienced. This testimony is fallible, however, partly because most of the survivors saw only a small part of this huge institution; partly because they had no way of recording events as they happened, under conditions of great hardship; partly because memory itself is fallible, and half-stifled recollections are still emerging fifty years after the war; partly because many of these memoirs have been worked on by interviewers, ghost writers and editors, whose contributions to the process are now inextricably intertwined with the raw material of raw memory.

One ends by making very subjective judgments about the spirit and reliability of each witness. Among the accounts I have found particularly impressive are: (1) *Survival in Auschwitz: The Nazi Assault on Humanity*, by Primo Levi, originally titled *Se Questo è un Uomo* (If this is a man), translated by Stuart Woolf (1958). A chemist by profession, Levi turned out to be a remarkable writer, combining the precision of a scientist and the sensitivity of a poet. He was confined on the periphery of Auschwitz, at the labor camp known as Buna, but his observations cover all the essentials of camp life. The success of this book was such that Levi wrote a series of sequels—notably *Moments of Reprieve, The Drowned and the Saved, The Reawakening, The Periodic Table*, and *If Not Now, When?*—before depression drove him to commit suicide in 1987. (2) *I Cannot Forgive*, by Rudolf Vrba and Alan Bestic (1964). Vrba, an intelligent and indomitable man, a chemist by profession, survived two years in Auschwitz, saw a great deal, finally escaped and brought important evidence to the Allies. (Bestic is the writer.) (3) *Five Chimneys, The Story of Auschwitz*, by Olga Lengyel (1947). A trained nurse and the wife of a Romanian psychiatrist, Mrs. Lengyel combines a rather sketchy account of the camp as a whole (one of the first to be published) with the much stronger story of her own efforts to organize the prisoner hospital. (4) *This Way for the Gas, Ladies and Gentlemen*, by Tadeusz Borowski, tr. Barbara Vedder (originally published in two collections of stories in Poland in 1948, translated into English in 1967, and now available in a Penguin paperback, 1976). A poet of considerable power, Borowski presented his stories as fiction, but they are clearly based on fact. The fictionalization enabled Borowski to blur the element of his own collaboration with the camp hierarchy, but that in turn strengthens the verisimilitude of the stories. Borowski became a police official in Poland's Stalinist regime before committing suicide in 1951. (5) *Hanged at Auschwitz*, by Sim Kessel, tr. Melville and Delight Wallace (1972). A tough and likable French boxer, arrested while smuggling arms, Kessel offers no remarkable insights but epitomizes the will to fight on.

Also extremely valuable in different ways are: (1) *The Death*

Factory: Documents on Auschwitz, by Ota Kraus and Erich Kulka, tr. Stephen Jolly (originally written in Czech and published in 1946 but revised and reprinted several times, most recently in London in 1966). Kraus and Kulka made a niche for themselves in Auschwitz as skilled craftsmen and repairmen. Then they began gathering other prisoners' recollections, which they assembled into an important though somewhat disorganized account of camp life. (2) *Man's Search for Meaning: An Introduction to Logotherapy,* by Viktor Frankl (1962, originally entitled *From Death-Camp to Existentialism*). This account, by an Austrian psychiatrist, is a perceptive analysis of how the SS methods destroyed the prisoners' identities and how that destruction could be resisted. (3) *Auschwitz: A Doctor's Eyewitness Account,* by Dr. Miklos Nyiszli, tr. Tibere Kremer and Richard Seaver (1960), and *Eyewitness Auschwitz: Three Years in the Gas Chambers,* by Filip Müller, ed. Helmut Freitag, tr. Susanne Flatauer (1979). A Hungarian pathologist, who was made an assistant to Dr. Mengele, and a Czech member of the *Sonderkommando* provide unique accounts of their coerced participation in the Final Solution. (4) *Fighting Auschwitz: The Resistance Movement in the Concentration Camp,* by Józef Garliński (1975). A prisoner himself but not a member of the underground, Garliński subsequently recreated the story of the Polish nationalist resistance.

Other noteworthy prisoner memoirs include (in alphabetical order): *At the Mind's Limits: Contemplations by a Survivor of Auschwitz,* by Jean Améry, tr. Sidney Rosenfeld and Stella P. Rosenfeld (1980); *Hope Is the Last to Die: A Personal Documentation of Nazi Terror,* by Halina Birenbaum, tr. David Walsh (1971); *None of Us Will Return,* by Charlotte Delbo, tr. John Githens (1968); *Playing for Time,* by Fania Fénelon with Marcelle Routier, tr. Judith Landry (1977); *I Am Alive,* by Kitty Hart (1961); *Night of the Mist,* by Eugène Heimler, tr. André Ungar (undated); *Anus Mundi: 1500 Days in Auschwitz/Birkenau,* by Wieslaw Kielar (1980); *In the Hell of Auschwitz: The Wartime Memoirs of Judith Sternberg Newman* (1963); *Night,* by Elie Wiesel, tr. Stella Rodway (1960).

More fragmentary but hardly less important are the statements of the survivors who testified in court against their persecutors. The most important collection is *Auschwitz: A Report on the Proceedings Against Robert Karl Mulka and Others before the Court at Frankfurt*, by Bernd Naumann, tr. Jean Steinberg (1966). This is an excellent account by a German journalist of the 1964 trial of two dozen Auschwitz officials, and I have quoted extensively from such witnesses as Ella Lingens and Otto Wolken. An impressive dramatic arrangement of this testimony was devised by Peter Weiss under the title *The Investigation* (1966). See also *Trial of Josef Kramer and Forty-Four Others (The Belsen Trial)*, ed. Raymond Phillips (1949). (Another noteworthy collection of memoirs, though not court testimony, is *Voices from the Holocaust*, ed. Sylvia Rothschild (1981) for the William E. Wiener Oral History Library of the American Jewish Committee.)

There is far less testimony from the Nazi side, of course, but Rudolf Hoess left a unique confession. Originally published in a Polish translation entitled *Wspomnienia* (1951), Hoess' story appeared in English as *Commandant of Auschwitz: The Autobiography of Rudolf Hoess*, tr. Constantine Fitzgibbon (1959). The chapters dealing with Auschwitz (about two thirds of the book) also appear in a valuable collection, *KZ Auschwitz as seen by the SS*, ed. Jadwiga Bezwińska and Danuta Czech (1972), which further includes the confessions of Perry Broad and the journal of Dr. Johann Paul Kremer. This book was published by the museum at Auschwitz, which continues to study and report on the documentary remnants of the camp, notably in fifteen volumes of records, analyses and recollections entitled *Zeszyty Oswiecimskie*, translated into German by Herta Henschel *et al.* under the title *Hefte von Auschwitz*. The museum's English-language works also include *Selected Problems from the History of KZ Auschwitz*, by Kazimierz Smoleń *et al.* (1979), and Smoleń's detailed *Guide-Book* (1978).

Despite the quantity of memoirs on Auschwitz, there is as yet no comprehensive book on the camp. Perhaps the nearest thing to it is *Concentration Camp Oswiecim-Brzezinka, Based on Documentary Evidence and Sources*, by Jan Sehn, tr. Klemens Keplics (1957). Sehn was the presiding judge at Hoess' trial before the Polish Supreme National Tribunal and at the subsequent trial of forty Auschwitz officials. Though rather terse and dry, his account gives considerable detail on Nazi activities and general living conditions in the camp.

Since Auschwitz was the center of the Holocaust, it naturally forms a major part in the many books on the disaster as a whole. On this, probably the most valuable studies are (in alphabetical order): *A History of the Holocaust*, by Yehuda Bauer (1982); *The War Against the Jews*, by Lucy S. Dawidowicz (1975); *The Holocaust: The History of the Jews of Europe during the Second World War*, by Martin Gilbert (1985); *The Destruction of the European Jews*, by Raul Hilberg (1961); *The Holocaust: The Destruction of European Jewry*, by Nora Levin (1973); *The Final Solution: The Attempt to Exterminate the Jews of Europe*, by Gerald Reitlinger (1953); and *The Holocaust: The Fate of European Jewry, 1933–1945*, by Leni Yahil (1990).

On various specific aspects of the Holocaust, I am indebted to *Eichmann in Jerusalem: A Report on the Banality of Evil*, by Hannah Arendt (1963, revised 1964); *The Crime and Punishment of I. G. Farben*, by Joseph Borkin (1976); *Less than Slaves: Jewish Forced Labor and the Quest for Compensation*, by Benjamin B. Ferencz (1979); *The Terrible Secret: Suppression of the Truth about Hitler's 'Final Solution,'* by Walter Laqueur (1980); *Auschwitz and the Allies*, by Martin Gilbert (1981); *They Fought Back: The Story of the Jewish Resistance in Nazi Europe*, ed. and tr. Yuri Suhl (1967); *The Murderers Among Us*, by Simon Wiesenthal, ed. Joseph Wechsberg (1967); *The Theory and Practice of Hell*, by Eugen Kogon (1946); *The Nazi Doctors: Medical Killing and the Psychology of Genocide*, by Robert Jay Lifton (1986); *The "Last" Nazi, The Life and Times of Dr. Joseph Mengele*, by Gerald Astor (1985); *The Survivor: An Anatomy of Life in the Death Camps*, by Terrence Des Pres (1976); *A Double Dying: Reflections on Holocaust Literature*, by Alvin H. Rosenfeld (1980); *The Holocaust and the Literary Imagination*, by Lawrence L. Langer (1975); *Inside the Vicious Heart: Americans and the Liberation of Nazi Concentration Camps*, by Robert H. Abzug (1985); *Auschwitz: Beginning of a New Era? Reflections* on the Holocaust, ed. Eva Fleischner (1977); *The Jewish Return into History, Reflections in the Age of Auschwitz and a New Jerusalem*, by Emil L. Fackenheim (1978); *Shoah, An Oral History of the Holocaust*, by Claude Lanzmann (1985); *The Abandonment of the Jews: America and the Holocaust, 1941–1945*, by David S. Wyman (1984); and *The Holocaust Kingdom* by Alexander Donat.

Index of Names